THE SPIRIT OF SHIANDA

BEHIND THE CLOAK OF CURSES

Based On Actual Events
CRYS SPEAKS

The Spirit of Shianda. Copyright 2021 by Crys Speaks. All rights reserved. No part of this publication may be reproduced, distributed, or transmitted in any form or by any means, including photocopying, recording, or other electronic or mechanical methods, without the prior written permission of the publisher, except in the case of brief quotations embodied in critical reviews and certain other noncommercial uses permitted by copyright law.

For permission requests, write to the publisher, addressed "Attention: Permissions Coordinator," 205 N. Michigan Avenue, Suite #810, Chicago, IL 60601. 13th & Joan books may be purchased for educational, business or sales promotional use. For information, please email the Sales Department at sales@13thandjoan.com.

Printed in the U. S. A.

First Printing, November 2021.

Library of Congress Cataloging-in-Publication Data has been applied for.

ISBN: 978-1-953156-48-8

www.CrysSpeaks.com

Dear Heavenly Father, I dedicate this book to you as an offering. You've saved my life from the strong grips of Satan and I owe everything to you. My first allegiance is to you. I proclaim to the nations that Jesus Christ is King. I pray that this sacrificial offering brings glory to your name and sets your people free.

"So have no fear of them, for nothing is covered that will not be revealed, or hidden that will not be known. What I tell you in the dark, say in the light, and what you hear whispered, proclaim on the housetops. And do not fear those who kill the body but cannot kill the soul. Rather fear him who can destroy both soul and body in hell."

—Matthew 10:26-28

A Foreword

As a prayer partner, sister, and friend I've sat back and watched people stand in awe of how Crys "just gets it." To have someone connect in spirit, understand exactly where the person is coming from, and deliver sound advice that speaks to their situation makes a person feel like they're not going insane and that they have finally been heard. True healing takes place when a person is heard. To be a great motivator and speaker, one has to be a great listener. I've witnessed many people talk more than they listen; so to see Crys possess the ability to do both is definitely a gift from God. This body of work showcases her ability to hear from the spirit of God and translate that to ordinary people.

What I love most about Crys is her boldness, honesty, and loyalty. She cuts no corners when it comes to delivering truth and this book is a testament to these very words. I've never met a single person who provides the level of support and encouragement she gives; when she has it in her mind to see you win she will be your biggest cheerleader. Crys will press you into becoming a better person, it's almost as if God has given her a download of your higher self and she will not quit until you walk into your purpose, even if it means putting you in a headlock and dragging you across the finish line. That's her love language. She's put a great level of love and devotion into composing *The Spirit of Shianda: Behind The Cloak of Curses*. God has shown her how His people are living beneath their birthright due to the curses over their lives and she is determined to provoke change.

What Crys portrays on her social media outlets is who she is in real life, hence why she is "The Queen of Keepin' It Real." Her genuine heart is not just seen in her actions but it's felt by everyone who has had the privilege to stand in her light. It's one thing for a person to speak words from their throne but to see a person come down and serve in pure humility, even in the washing of feet, is impeccable. I am not just referring to communion, it's a lifestyle for her. The level of transparency in this book about her personal life experiences showcases her willingness to bare all for the sake of healing God's people. Healing flows through her and she is generous with healing others from all walks of life. Whether your neck or heart is aching, Crys will be there nursing you right back to health. She's literally a seed of Christ. She shows the utmost compassion but will flip a few tables if necessary. This too is transcended in her writing.

Crys innately has a maternal and nurturing nature. I know God put that inside of her to birth nations. I am proud of the woman she has become in Christ and her obedience to the call in spite of adversity. I am positive that this book will cut like a double-edged sword, but for those who desire change it will prepare them to defeat the giants in their lives through the power of Christ Jesus. Living in a world where busyness is the norm, this book challenges readers to turn their attention from the world they can see and begin to focus more on the unseen world - the spirit realm. What I love most is that this book gives instructions on how to overcome. It's backed by the word of God and it is written in a way where even a child could understand it. I know that is the way Christ would want it. It tears down the walls of traditions and exposes Satan's tricks and schemes.

I believe there will be a great rise of God's people in these last days. Believers will not look like your typical "Christians" but will have God's undeniable power resting upon their lives. As her sister and friend I have experienced the trials of life she speaks of in this book with her and watched her press into God for deliverance. As a believer, this book boosted my confidence in Christ, reassuring me that I don't have to walk according to man but according to the laws of God. I always knew the calling over Crys' life was major, but this body of work has exceeded my expectations. I am confident that God's words, which are outlined in this book, will activate readers' spiritual understanding and provoke them to break the curses over their lives and walk in true freedom.

Chanice L.
President, Respect My Call Inc.
Co-Owner, 31 Corridor LLC
www.31corridor.com

Contents

A FOREWORD VII

PREFACE 1

INTRODUCTION 5

CHAPTER 1
"I thought I would become a pioneer but ended up a prisoner."
Traded My Blessings for Curses 7

CHAPTER 2
"The witchcraft behind secret societies."
Exposing the World of the Occult 13

CHAPTER 3
"Revelation from God."
The Spirit of Shianda #5 37

CHAPTER 4
"I'm going to church but not growing."
Information Without Application is Useless 49

CHAPTER 5
"You can't wear the cloak of clergy and the cloak of curses at the same time. Pick a side. Choose life or death"
The Cloak of Curses 51

CHAPTER 6
"The elect of God has been deceived by the elite of this world."
Stolen Identity 56

JOURNAL ENTRY 72

JOURNAL ENTRY 76

CHAPTER 7
"The curses they brought upon themselves fell on me."
Generational Curses 78

CHAPTER 8
"Realigning with God's will."
Getting Out 84

JOURNAL ENTRY 87

CHAPTER 9
"Don't touch my hair."
The Curses Levied On The Crown 92

CHAPTER 10
"Dreams are the eye-gate into the spiritual world."
Nothing Happens Physically before Being Spiritually Conceived 96

CHAPTER 11
"Time to take action."
Breaking the Curses 100

ACKNOWLEDGEMENTS 117

AFTERWORD: 119

WORKS CITED 129

GLOSSARY 133

Preface

I posted a twenty-two-minute video sharing part of my testimony on social media. The video went viral. It spoke of my involvement with the occult world through my membership with a popular Black Greek Letter Organization. It revealed the deceptive nature of secret societies, how my life turned upside down, and compelled others to come out while there was still time. There was an outpouring of love and appreciation from people. The fans pushed the video day and night, sharing it with family, friends, and coworkers who are actively in the world of the occult and even with people who had entertained the idea of joining. I had multiple people openly share their testimonies, alongside receiving emails from members of secret societies who wanted out immediately, given the newly discovered information I provided in the video. They felt deceived and ashamed just as I had and needed instruction on how to get out physically and spiritually. God had given me the command to free His people and I was determined to do just that. With over 700 recorded videos to encourage others, God was now pushing me to write. There was a message that needed to be delivered to His people and my life had served as a sacrifice so that others would not have to stay with their struggles.

    I was very vocal and proud when crossing into the world of the occult. I vowed to God to be just as vocal with my experience of getting out, in order to help bring folks out of the house of bondage. While it is true that we live in a rebellious society, the sad reality is that many are bound by curses that they have been deceived into or inherited. Witchcraft is all around us. Secret societies run the world and much of what is seen by the human eye is an augmented reality. Through divine impartation, God has unveiled to me the tricks and schemes of the enemy and has prophesied much of what will take place on this Earth. What is taking place in our waking life has already been conceived spiritually. It will take spiritual warfare to combat the enemy's wiles and release the blessings of God. That is what this book discusses.

As I endeavored to create this book, God began to give me words to write quicker than I could actually regurgitate them. But as always, the enemy was out to shut down the great work which had begun. I had multiple attacks levied against me and they were heavy. Several passages of information were lost due to software issues. I had properly saved the document and just like that, it disappeared when I tried to access the file the following day. There were no traces of my autosaves or previously saved files either. The devil was busy, but God continued to encourage me through dreams and impartations. The more I progressed with the book the more spiritual attacks came through dreams. One dream entailed a man dressed in all black seeking to pry my mouth open to rip out my tongue. Yes, Satan wanted me silent. I broke free from the dream by calling on the name of Jesus. In a different dream, a woman who was a witch wore all black and said, "I will give you what you want, just give him what he wants." This demonic force was offering to give me whatever I desired as long as I granted Satan his wish for me to be silent. I was facing opposition spiritually and physically. It was as if Satan's agents were put on alert and were aiming their attacks directly at me. My body felt as if it were taking blows by the hour, but I still knew that God was with me.

The Holy Spirit gave me the book of Isaiah chapter 60 in a dream. He confirmed that if I stayed on course and completed my assignment then Isaiah 60 would be the heritage of His people. "Nations will come to your light, and kings to the brightness of your dawn. Lift up your eyes and look about you: All assemble and come to you; your sons come from afar and your daughters are carried on the hip ... The least of you will become a thousand, the smallest a mighty nation. I am the Lord; in its time I will do this swiftly."

The Lord made me aware that time was of the essence, so I wrote this book anywhere and everywhere. I had no scheduled time or place to write. Wherever God gave the revelation I wrote. I would write in line at the grocery store, waking up from a dream, or walking to my car; and I constantly texted and emailed myself notes to ensure that everything was accounted for. I received a great deal of revelation through conversation and I gritted my teeth until this book was complete. The best gift is to receive the gift of life through Christ. I urge you to hear what God is saying and govern yourself accordingly.

I WILL NOT SIT AND ALLOW THE PEOPLE OF GOD TO LIVE IN BONDAGE WHEN OUR BIRTHRIGHT IS FREEDOM

Ephesians 5:6-14: Let no one deceive you with empty words, for because of these things the wrath of God comes upon the sons of disobedience. Therefore do not become partners with them; for at one time you were darkness, but now you are light in the Lord. Walk as children of light (for the fruit of light is found in all that is good and right and true), and try to discern what is pleasing to the Lord. ..

I WILL USE MY VOICE TO REVEAL TO OTHERS WHAT GOD HAS REVEALED TO ME THROUGH HIS SPIRIT

Deuteronomy 29:29 "The secret things belong to the Lord our God, but the things that are revealed belong to us and to our children forever, that we may do all the words of this law.

Introduction

Have you ever gotten to a place in your life where everything was falling apart? A place where you're left wondering, "how did I get here?" Well I've definitely been there. The lack that I was experiencing in my life was not ordinary. In fact, it made no sense at all. How does a person who "follows the rules of life" still end up failing? For years I fought the idea that God hated me to a certain degree, and that His will for my life was for me to fail. Or maybe He gave His toughest soldiers the hardest fight? Perhaps I was supposed to go through hell and high water to serve as a testimony to others. Could it be that if I suffered long enough on Earth that I would make it into heaven on the account of grace and endurance? I loved the Lord. I believed with all my whole heart that Jesus Christ was my personal Lord and savior. I did as much as I could and knew to live "upright." As much as I tried to keep the faith, clearly something was not adding up in my life because at the onset of my adulthood I found myself in a constant cycle of backwardness and stagnancy. *Lord, where is my harvest?* This question plagued my mind and spirit for years. Many of us have walked through life doing the best we knew how with people, our finances, our jobs, and in our relationships, but always seem to come up short. Unbeknownst to me, my harvest was being devoured by the spirits I was harvesting on the inside of me.

Unfortunately, I lived a life of spiritual ignorance. As the Bible teaches, "every man is justified in his own eyes" according to the book of Proverbs chapter 21 verse 2. I had no idea that the perfect life I planned out for myself would be abruptly interrupted by the Spirit of Shianda. Did I know that there was a demonic force controlling my life as my life spiraled out of control? No. Did I work to the point of exhaustion to fix what was broken? Of course. Everything inside of me is a fighter, but with this battle, I had no hands, I was tied up. Was I physically in chains? No, but I lived my life as a slave to demons that were assigned to hinder and block the blessings preordained for my life. There were covenants I made and evil altars I was bound to. I was entangled in a powerful system of witchcraft with no understanding. I was walking down a road set ablaze by a false light, one that would lead to spiritual and physical destruction.

For me, ignorance did not remain bliss, it became torturous, frustrating, and dark. I've never been arrested, convicted of a crime, or taken to jail, but I was a prisoner in the worst way. I was imprisoned spiritually. We are physical beings fighting a spiritual warfare that we cannot see. Yet many of our lives show how badly we've been losing this battle. The truth is, the covenants we've made in ignorance could be the very factors that keep us spiritually and physically restricted in all areas of our lives.

Now we are about to get into the nitty-gritty. The details outlined provide answers to topics that are typically shied away from due to their controversial nature, like the world of witchcraft, secret societies, governmental control, the untold history of the Black presence in the Bible —a stolen culture which has augmented reality for many Blacks, spiritual warfare, and the dream world. I want to unveil to you a system deeply knitted in the kingdom of darkness that influences your life directly and indirectly whether you know it or not. This book is meant to provoke you to think differently about the information presented to you on a daily basis. No longer should you accept things blindly, I mean nothing. I need you to understand the evil unseen forces that are controlling the physical world we live in, in order to enhance your spiritual journey and make it out of this matrix. We should no longer look at anything for mere face value, but instead test everything by the Holy Spirit and the word of the true and living God. Deception is real, but this book provides you a door out of the world of bondage and directs you to a pathway that leads to true freedom and eternal life.

I

"I thought I would become a pioneer but ended up a prisoner."

TRADED MY BLESSINGS FOR CURSES

Do you believe in curses, magic, the unseen? Now tell me, do you believe in blessings? In this twisted world that we live in, many people believe in one and not the other. Truth be told, both curses and blessings exist. Imagine this truth: there are blessings set aside in the heavenly realms for your life, and there are curses that can stop those blessings from ever manifesting on Earth. The goal of Satan is to deceive you into creating an altar unto him so that he can alter who you were created to be. I do not know many people who would openly worship Satan. He deceives people into worshipping him by masking himself as various false gods, oftentimes through Greek letter organizations.

During my sophomore year of college, I became a member of Delta Sigma Theta Sorority, Incorporated. I had no clue that my greatest achievement would lead me to a long road of destruction. I can remember the day like it was yesterday, my heart was pounding. A line of twenty-eight young ladies had accomplished a lifelong dream. We finally joined the ranks of the most prestigious and sophisticated women in the world. This was the moment where we were presented to those who anticipated our arrival. It was springtime. The height of probate season on our campus. There were thousands of people including students, faculty, family, and friends in attendance waiting to witness the reveal of the most anticipated line. Some traveled from miles away to experience this very moment. It was exactly two years since the last line of Deltas crossed and my line was filled with the most influential women on campus. The music was blasting through the speakers and it felt like a championship. We were underground for months with little to no communication with outsiders. The time had finally arrived for us to be unleashed.

I felt like I was a part of a powerful army. There were twenty-eight of us dressed identically from head to toe. Red blouses, black slacks, black heels, and crimson and cream masks with our respective numbers. Our prophytes, also known as big sisters, were dressed in all white with red hats. They strutted in before us and our Ma Duck, also known as the Dean of Pledges, stayed close with her staff leading all twenty-eight of us into the outdoor amphitheater. As we got closer to the crowd and walked onto the ramp, the crowd erupted. We were on a whole nother level. The level of support was unreal. The respect was evident, we were undeniably a crowd favorite, and we were ready to give them the best show they had seen all semester. Other Greek organizations came to support us and were ready to welcome us with gifts and love to Greek life. Needless to say, we put on an amazing show. At the end of the show, I could remember greeting my friends and family and feeling like God, I finally made it.

I was having the time of my life in this new space. To be honest, I loved it! At the time, I was too busy to fully grasp the concept of what was taking place in my life. I was just excited to have finally made it over into "Delta Land." My mentors back home were proud of me. My status changed. I went from Crystal, the cool chick from Miami to *Crystal the Delta*. I loved being in a higher position yet humble enough to kick it with folks who were not Greek. There were parties every other night to go to and as neophytes, our presence had to be known. I remember getting my line shirt and later putting on my line jacket for the first time, both were glorious moments for me. If nothing else was right in my life, I had accomplished something that many only dreamed of. I officially crossed over to being the elite.

CRYS SPEAKS

My line sisters and I prepared for various step shows, hosted philanthropic events, programmed for the campus, held the highest leadership positions collectively, served within the community, and was all about Delta business. All day and all night we stayed busy working for Delta. I had a deep care for many of my line sisters and through all the hell we went through, at least I felt there were a few that I genuinely considered lifelong friends. We all understood that we were family no matter how dysfunctional we were at times. We road tripped, connected with other Sorors and chapters, and experienced what it meant to be the cream of the crop in the eyes of those who wished to be in our positions. Straight up, once I became Greek, privileges changed. No more standing in line to get into places, free drinks at the club, strolling just to show how much fun it was to be a Delta girl, and of course, the heightened male attention comes along with the territory. People who I had never even met knew me. Certain positions on campus became easier to attain and on top of that, I was now connected to thousands of boss women. So in many regards, I felt like I was living the dream. Delta was my life and anything outside of that was secondary, including God, church, family, and non-Greek friends. My prophytes made a point to always remind us of what our priorities should be, but it was virtually impossible for me to juggle all that and be a great Delta at the same time. This is just how Satan does, he allows you to experience high highs before hitting rock bottom. He distracts you with pleasure just to lead you into poverty. Proverbs 21:17 states, "He that loveth pleasure shall *be* a poor man." I came to find out that everything that glitters ain't gold.

What I saw as a blessing ended up being a curse. I realized that my life began to spiral out of control. It didn't just start post-college. In fact there were many red flags that I ignored. During the timeframe of my initiation, I begin to lose my ability to remember even the slightest things, especially the organization's historical information. I found it strange. From my youth, I have always identified with having the gift of memorization and speech. As a child, my mother enrolled me in oratorical contests, and they all seemed to be a breeze. This was undoubtedly a blessing. I never thought much of my blessings until they were attacked. I was a vivid dreamer my entire life up to that point, yet I did not dream the entire process as I pursued Delta. When you don't sleep you can't dream; moreover, when you are out of the will of God and living in sin, He tends to grow silent. I see now that my connection to the spirit of God was cut off, causing me to not operate in the gift of prophecy through dreams. It's impossible to listen to two masters, and God is not in the business of competing.

Crazier things began to happen. My identity was stolen while pledging for Delta, and I had to get permission to go home to get the situation sorted out. Turns out my mother ordered a copy of my social security card and while en route, the mail was intercepted. The thieves established small businesses in my name, had lights turned on at a home not far from my hometown's residential address, and began to live it up on my established credit. There were lawyers, interviews, and police reports conducted and the process seemed never-ending. Although I was not in the city where these transactions were made, I was fighting just to prove that I was really me. That was an unbelievable experience and a complete struggle. Can you see the instant downward effect or should I say more? For the sake of details, I'll say more. My grades began to drop and I withdrew from some of my college courses to avoid failing the semester and losing scholarships altogether. Plain and simple, I could not balance, and it felt like a force was driving my life. I was no longer in control no matter what I did to "stabilize." But I had taken an oath not to quit no matter what confronted me. I didn't realize it then, but the roots of witchcraft had begun to affect me because of the evil covenant I unknowingly came into agreement with. I was under serious mind control. Physical exhaustion and mental confusion are key indicators while under the influence of mind control. I had no clue about this because I was deeply immersed in the world of witchcraft. Through the ups and downs, I somehow managed to graduate with a Bachelor's degree, nonetheless life began to worsen.

CRYS SPEAKS

A DEGREE BUT FACING DEPRESSION

There is nothing more heartbreaking than standing face to face with yourself in the mirror and seeing a complete failure. Many of us have done everything we know in our power to be right, only to end up wrong. What I hate most is that when folks paint the perfect picture of success it usually involves working hard, staying out of trouble, achieving the highest level of academic success, joining the right organizations, networking with the right people, and *voila*, just like that you too could be living the "American Dream." For me, life quickly determined that that was a lie. Publicly, I kept a smile on my face and was an "it girl," but it seemed the more I worked and labored, the more I failed. The little bit of success I experienced could not begin to accommodate for the pitfalls. Through my silent battles, I maintained a quality social image, but behind closed doors, life was plummeting quickly. I had no way of managing. After a car repossession, homelessness, an extreme attack on my skin and scalp, physical deterioration, strained relationships with my family, and overall impoverishment, I really began to think that God hated me and living became torturous. After a while, my degree was nothing more than an expensive piece of paper. I stayed away from my sorority sisters because I felt no connection as if I did not belong; we seemed to be on different paths. As a person who is big on love, I just didn't feel it from those I expected it from.

There were high school dropouts further ahead in life than I was. It was the most embarrassing part of my life. The hardest part about losing everything was feeling like I did everything in my power to bulletproof myself from failure only to end up in an unrecognizable predicament. My circumstance just did not make sense, so I concluded that God had it out for me. Something inside of me knew that with the number of gifts and talents I possessed, there was no way I should be in this situation. I took matters into my own hands because prayers weren't working. I contemplated delving into manifestation. I even went as far as purchasing a journal to incept my ideas and go full-fledged into it. This may be a jaw-dropper for some but hey it was my reality. Desperate times can cause you to do desperate things. The life of a Christian wasn't profiting me. I was determined to find another way. I told my prayer partner my plans and she instantly rebuked the unclean spirit that was trying to influence me to turn my back on the things of God.

I was broken. Hope was lost in every way. I was troubled in my spirit. My world consisted of low points physically, spiritually, and emotionally. I resulted in taking dead-end jobs to survive as most places I sought employment with said I was overqualified. These atmospheres were loud, negative, and primarily consisted of recovering addicts. I had no idea how I ended up there, and minute by minute it chipped away at my confidence. As a person who is big on cleanliness, it frustrated me that I always seemed to be surrounded by the filth at my jobs and in the places I rented. All of the places that I rented had septic issues and reeked of sewage, but after all, that was what I could afford. I was not welcomed in any of my immediate family members' homes. One went as far as calling me a beggar, another blocked my number, others gossiped about me. I kept my distance to maintain my sanity. The life of poverty had truly set in.

2

"The Witchcraft Behind Secret Societies."
EXPOSING THE WORLD OF THE OCCULT

During this period I found myself crying out to God with the help and support of my prayer partner. God began to minister to me in dreams. Some dreams were straight forward while others did not make much sense to me at the time. One night while sleeping, the Lord revealed "The Spirit of Shianda" to me with the number five. The words were very clear, I heard the annunciation of the name and could see it spelled. I made a habit of writing my dreams down in great detail so that I could easily recall them. I had no idea whether this dream in particular was good or bad so I asked God for revelation because I did not need any more uncertainties in my life. I continued studying the word of God, trying to survive day by day in the whirlwind. At that time, I was not aware that God was revealing to me what had me bound.

The more I sought God, the more He revealed to me names of spirits, colors, and numbers. I dreamt so much during that period that by the morning I felt as if I hadn't slept at all. This was my daily routine. Anyone who knows me knows I don't play about my food or sleep, but I kept pressing God because I knew He was revealing something. I just could not understand it. One month and five days after I received the dream regarding the Spirit of Shianda, I was asked by a friend to watch a video that would change the course of my life. I was sitting in the code enforcement office getting paperwork processed. It was a long wait and I decided to watch it because I needed to pass time while in the lobby. This video was one that exposed the truth behind the "Divine 9" organizations. For those who do not know what the Divine 9 is, it is a group of nine historically Black Greek Letter Organizations which are portrayed as "Christian-based" groups committed to sisterhood/brotherhood, service, academic excellence, and the betterment of the Black community. As previously mentioned, I was a part of the Divine 9 through my membership with Delta Sigma Theta Sorority, Incorporated. This was the season I was ready to receive the truth because prior to that day, I had aggressively rejected any and everyone who seemed to be in opposition to my beloved sorority. I was known to defend my sorority with my life, after all, not everyone could be one of us and for those who were chosen, we worked extremely hard to be a part of that prestigious and sophisticated organization.

In the video I watched, there was a young lady who had joined Zeta Phi Beta Sorority, Incorporated, another Divine 9 organization. This woman spoke out revealing the hidden truths behind these secret societies. She posed various thought-provoking questions and backed her answers with supporting biblical scriptures. She asked, if these organizations are in fact based upon Christian principles, then why would there be a need for a patron of an organization? Why are the songs and chants designed to give praise to these patrons? As soon as the video ended, I shouted "I WANT OUT!" I was utterly disgusted. Anger bubbled from the inner depths of me. I felt betrayed by what they had done to me in deception, yet broken from what I had done to God. My day shifted and my mind was no longer on work. I rushed to wrap up what I was doing and hurried to get to my Delta ritual book and doctrine. That video provoked me to research what I had willingly bound myself to. I did not have a split second of doubt. I was determined to get out of the cult I joined masked as a sisterhood. I found in my own research that I had been deceived into serving another god practicing in Pagan worship. The greatest shock to me was that I had become a witch and didn't even know it.

My spiritual eye gate was open and there was no way I could deny what had been hidden in plain sight. Satan has such great power and exudes it cunningly. He masks in the likeness of God to deceive the people of God. Satan mimics everything of Christ and his disciples follow suit. "And no marvel, for Satan himself is transformed into an angel of light." reads 2 Corinthians 11:14. The self-proclaimed "illuminated ones" have a way of drawing the elect of God into their false light. The true light of the world are the disciples of Christ. Matthew 5:14-16 states, "You are the light of the world. A town built on a hill cannot be hidden. Neither do people light a lamp and put it under a bowl. Instead, they put it on its stand, and it gives light to everyone in the house. In the same way, let your light shine before others, that they may see your good deeds and glorify your Father in heaven." They draw us in deceptively so that we abandon our God and glorify their god, Satan.

I know many who have seen the obvious in regard to these organizations for years are probably asking, how could you not know? Let me tell you, the deceit blended so well that I was pulled in more and more each day through the good works we did in the community and the biblical scriptures we referenced in ceremonies. I took what was written to heart. After all, these organizations are "based on Christian principles." Satan is the author of lies who has been deceiving even the elect of God's people. He was persuasive enough to convince one-third of the angels to join him in his rebellion (Revelation 12:4). Now, what do you think happens to mere human beings? These angels were in the presence of God and still were able to be persuaded by Satan. So just because you go to church and pray doesn't mean you're exempt from falling into Satan's schemes. Satan is very powerful. He did not like being "second best." He wanted to be God.

> *"You said in your heart, 'I will ascend to heaven; I will raise my throne above the stars of God; I will sit enthroned on the mount of assembly, on the utmost heights of the sacred mountain'"*
Isaiah 14:13. This was the beginning of sin and the root of witchcraft.

Now that we have a clear understanding of just how powerful and persuasive Satan is, let's delve into his schemes. Being discreet is the label given to living an abominable life in secrecy. Make no mistake, God instructs us to practice discretion but never to live a life of secrecy. After all, nothing is hidden before God. These secret societies that run the world swindle their members into becoming accustomed to living a secret life covering downfalls through an external portrayal of success at the cost of their soul. Once God breaks you from the cloak of curses you will easily identify the plots and schemes of Satan manifested in the world around us. This includes the government, televised news, sitcoms, award shows, etc. This world as we know it operates off of rituals and ceremonies. I too was a blind participant, as most of the world at large is. As I studied, God revealed to me the witchcraft I engaged in during my entanglement with the world of the occult.

What I am about to reveal are dark hidden secrets. I am not afraid of the "powers that be" because my Father in heaven has already ordered divine protection over my life. Matthew 10:26-28 states, "So have no fear of them, for nothing is covered that will not be revealed, or hidden that will not be known. What I tell you in the dark, say in the light, and what you hear whispered, proclaim on the housetops. And do not fear those who kill the body but cannot kill the soul. Rather fear him who can destroy both soul and body in hell."

The Holy Spirit began to show me the candle magic, altars, and tools that were used to usher me into the world of darkness. Just as with any contract, there is an offer and acceptance. After the rush, the formal informational setting, I completed my application for Delta. The application and my interview along with my credentials were suitable enough for the chapter I was pursuing to offer me an invitation to pursue membership into their exclusive group. Feeling in my soul that this would be the very thing to launch me into a higher level of life, I accepted the offer and the journey began. What I didn't know is that I would be a participant in higher-level magic.

During my induction ceremony into Delta as a pyramid, I remember being dressed in all white. Each of us pursuing Delta looked exactly the same from head to toe as uniformity was key. We were led out from the foyer area of a church to the inside sanctuary. All twenty-eight of us filed into the pews on the left side. We entered the pitch-black sanctuary. The only visible light came from penlights held by the Minerva Circle members and the wick candles set ablaze on tables. Directly in front of us were the Minerva Circle members draped in crimson robes, behind a table decorated with various items. A white tablecloth with the Greek letters Delta Sigma Theta dressed the table skirt. It was quiet, dramatic, and quite intimidating. You could hear a pin drop if one would dare. Women of Delta who included previous chapter members and supporting Sorors from near and far filled the right side of the room, clothed in all black with some form of pin displaying the Greek letters or with the organization's official flower, the African violet. It was located on the outermost layer of their clothing. I had not experienced anything like it, I don't believe any of us had. The chapter president's voice who presided over the ceremony was commanding.

Throughout parts of the ceremony, music played and a series of messages resounded. I watched twenty-seven young ladies go, one by one before me. Kneeling on a white pillow and clasping their hands around a red candle representing the torch of wisdom, state their name and swear by the pledge listed on the scroll. They all signed the contract before them. I was up next. When I got to the table to kneel, I was so uneasy, but I hurried up and did what I had to do because twenty-seven other brave young women had already done it. I was the last in line. Although I had time to escape, I wouldn't dare. I was not about to stop the ceremony. We were one step closer to advancing forward in Delta.

The spells were in the words of the poetry spoken, the incantations in the words of the songs we sang, and the oath that we took. The red and white burning candles strategically placed in the holder shaped like the Greek letter Sigma were tools used to light the flames and usher the spirits of false gods to fill that place. Just as I had come before the altar of God many times before, seeking Him and asking for His Spirit to be poured out on me, I had done the same thing but this time to Minerva, the goddess and patron of Delta Sigma Theta. The sad part is that I did not know it. Even in one of the prayers we sang as Deltas, it states, "oh heavenly Father pour on us thy spirit, send us thy blessings in this hour with thee." The Father was Satan, the governing force behind Minerva.

At that ceremony, we were each individually pinned by a member of Delta who had come to see us or by a special sister in the chapter. We were instructed to put our right hand over our heart and separate our pinky fingers. That would be the place where we were pinned with a gold pyramid. The pyramid pin would be worn over our hearts on our innermost garments every day of our process until we officially became Delta women. That didn't ring any alarm to me because after all, I had pledged allegiance to the flag of the United States of America all twelve years of school. In my mind, there was no difference. I would later come to know I had undertaken an oath long before my pursuit of Delta as many of us have. I had already pledged under the grand system of Satanists disguised as the "founding fathers" of the land we were brought into as captives hundreds of years ago, "America the Great." As pyramids, we were compliant then just as we had all been as students in pursuit of education in prior years. The hand over heart is a symbol used in Satanic and Masonic practices.

"Masonry's honor to the heart by the sign of hand on heart can best be understood by the fact that the leaders of the Masonic Lodge themselves boast that the rituals of Freemasonry hearken back to ancient Egyptian religion. The Egyptian Book of the Dead addressed prayers to "My heart of my mother... My heart of transformation," meaning the source of rebirths. The Mother Goddess of Egypt was worshipped by various names — Isis, Hathor, Rhea, etc. She was the one to whom the people "gave their hearts," meaning their heartfelt devotion and allegiance, their FIDELITY. As the Goddess of sacrifices, it was deemed necessary by her admirers that men should sacrifice their "energies" on her behalf.

The Goddess was said to take possession of the hearts of men." (Codex Magica) It is no coincidence that Delta's fifth cardinal virtue (5, like the number of fingers) is fidelity which is one's loyalty or steadfast devotion to the Goddess Minerva masked as Satan. Additionally, "In the pyramids of Mexico, Central and South America, the gods were also gods of sacrifice and, once again, the heart was the centerpiece of devotion. Bloodthirsty followers, egged on by high priests, cut out the hearts of tribal war victims and ate them." (The Pyramids of Mexico)

In the United States, Marine corps' hand over heart ceremonies are called blood pinning in the tradition known as blood wings. In many sectors of the armed forces, graduates have the pins and badges slammed into the graduate's chest resulting in the pins being driven into the flesh. (Blood Wings) It has been said that blood wings are against armed forces rules but are done in secret much like hazing in Greek-letter organizations. These are all occult practices. All of us had become blood sacrifices unto an altar erected unto Satan the night of our induction. There is no wonder why God says, "above all else, guard your heart, for everything you do flows from it," Proverbs 4:23. Jesus himself was pierced and nailed to the cross, becoming the blood sacrifice for the curse of sin. Satan initiated us back over into the cloak of curses by pinning us to his altar.

Just as the government is built on branches, all Greek-letter organizations are divided into different branches and subdivisions of the Illuminati under the authority of Satan. We were all a part of the body serving a different purpose unto Satan. Hence why you see Minerva holding the laurel wreath or olive branch. That symbolizes all of her members' (Deltas) place in Satan's Kingdom. In the beginning, Scripture teaches us in the book of Genesis about the tree of good and evil. God forbade Adam and Eve to eat off the tree, according to Genesis 2:17: "But of the tree of the knowledge of good and evil you shall not eat, for in the day that you eat of it you shall surely die." People are awake but die spiritually every day based upon the evil covenants they make. As most are familiar with the story, we know Satan deceived Adam and Eve into disobeying

God which resulted in them being cursed and thrown out of the Garden of Eden. Christ who became the curse is the "Tree of Life." He is our life source. If Christ is the tree and we are in the body of Christ, then we are divided into branches of the tree. His children all serve different purposes but still are connected to the body, sent to fulfill his plan. "Now you are the body of Christ, and members individually." -1 Corinthians 12:27.

I became a member of Satan's tree of evil. The kingdom of Satan is here on Earth, he represents the tree of evil. He has built a governmental system full of occult practices. Hence why the government is made up of three "branches:" legislative, executive, and judicial, that connect to the source of Satan. He is infiltrating the God-head, the Father, Son, and Holy Spirit. There is no surprise that many of these world leaders and entertainers are connected to the world of the occult. While in Delta, I represented a pyramid and the eye of Providence (Satan) which are both symbols located on the money we carry and made by our government system. We carry these occult articles with us not even understanding their origins. It is no surprise that God would say, "for the love of money is the root of all kinds of evil." Satan understood who God gave jurisdiction over the Earth and what his adversary would use to coerce God's people back into bondage. The Bible confirms this: "when they brought the coin, and He (Jesus) asked them, 'Whose image is this? And whose inscription?' 'Caesar's,' they replied. 'Give back to Caesar what is Caesar's and to God what is God's.'" Mark 12:16-17. Caesar's source was Satan. This system that we live in is built on Satanic principles which form the Illuminati. Pyramids symbolize the levels that lead to the higher archery of the kingdom of Satan. The higher you are, the more earthly power you have. Black Greek Letter Organizations are a part of this system as well.

Let's revisit the induction ceremony. As it continued, I remember shedding tears when the Big Sisters created a huge circle around us and we all sang the "Pyramid Hymn" together in unison. At the time I believed it to be a beautiful moment and very overwhelming. There was undeniable energy raised in the room and I felt it to my core. The women we researched were now in our presence, surrounding us, and willing to bring us into a sisterhood of "excellence." Some traveled for hundreds of miles to see us and groom us into the best Deltas we could be. In the same way, Jesus drew crowds as a healer. Large crowds came to hear Jesus speak. The Bible tells us that the crowds gathered around Him. In essence, they formed a circle around Him. Jesus' disciples gathered around Him throughout the journey of Jesus's mission, to listen to His teachings. They also gathered around Him as armor bearers (guards/protection) when he traveled preaching the word of God to the crowds. Although Jesus was all-powerful, His disciples were still put in the position to serve as protection with the crowds that came to see Him. There are several scriptures that speak of the disciples' interaction with the crowds. As Jesus was the centerpiece of the circles formed around Him by these large crowds and by His disciples, it is a display of His infinite power. Miracles took place within these circles. Satan uses the same concept. In occult practices, they form circles for energy, protection, and to usher in evil spirits.

Circles are formed at every ceremony in Delta. "A magic circle is a circle of space marked out by practitioners of ritual magic that contain energy and form a sacred space or provide them a form of magical protection, or both." (Magic Circle) While in many of these energy circles, another common ritual is unity hand-fasting rituals. Handfasting is known for the binding of two lives. This is something that is done with the singing of songs in these energy circles. Whether good or bad, energy is felt. It's a vibration that raises so strongly that even people outside the circle can feel it permeating, which draws spectators into this false light. During celebratory times, the "Sweetheart's Song" is chanted in a circle while a sway is introduced at a particular time in the song. The celebrated member(s) are in the center and other Sorors surround them forming a circle. The song states, "but if she wears the Delta symbol then her first love is DST." Now how can I claim to love God but profess that my first love is DST? Revelation 2 says, "you have turned from your first love." My first love should be Jesus Christ, anything else is considered idolatry.

With that in mind let's take a look at what members of the occult world practice. "Alchemy is defined as a medieval chemical science and speculative philosophy aiming to achieve the transmutation of the base metals into gold, the discovery of a universal cure for diseases, and the discovery of a means of indefinitely prolonging life." (Alchemy.) Satan is trying to duplicate Jesus the Healer and alter the natural course of life. "This too can be seen in the Indian philosophy Bindu. The Circle with a dot in the center is a representation of the sun, Egyptian 'sun god' (Ra), an archangel named Kabbalah, emotional restraint and divine consciousness of a universal god." A circled dot is Alchemy. The dot in the circle is said to represent the merging of female and male power. Earth-centric cults see the circle as a sacred space. This representation is also depicted as a serpent eating its own tail. Worshipped by many Earth-centric and Pagan cults, the serpent represents rebirth ... primarily because of its shedding of old skin. It is said to also represent the life force of females." (Satanic/Occult Symbols and Their Meanings) It is worth noting that Minerva can also be seen with a coiled serpent representing wisdom. We were all participating in ritualistic ceremonies unto false gods and there is no denying that.

This system that we live in starts us off early with brainwashing us while in circles through childhood nursery rhymes and games like Duck Duck Goose, Ring Around the Rosie, and even movies that remind us of the circle of life evolution such as *The Lion King*. These meta folklores are created to glorify Satan. Unbeknownst to innocent children and parents, they are reciting incantations created by witches and warlocks to raise energy and cast spells. Satan desires the hearts of the pure which is why children are targeted at an early age. Satan uses anyone who will further his mission to manipulate the will of God. Parents have sung "lullabies" to their children to help them sleep without understanding the origin of the word lullaby itself.

"Lullaby" is a derivative from Jewish folklore meaning "lilith abi," which in the English tongue simply means "Lilith, go away." Lilith, a she-demon, was said to have been Adam's first wife before Eve, so the term "lullaby" was coined in order to protect children from her. Throughout history, lullabies and nursery rhymes have been used as educational tools to teach children about morality, history, and proper behavior. Over time, the term "lullaby" stuck, and we now think of it as a soothing song used to calm children. However, history shows us that some lullabies are anything but soothing and are, in fact, horrifying if you understand their origin and know-how to read between the lines.

"RING AROUND THE ROSIE"

"Ring Around the Rosie, pocket full of posies, ashes, ashes, we all fall down!" This nursery rhyme references The Black Death in Europe, a bubonic plague pandemic that lasted from 1346 to 1352. The plague's appearance was black sores on the bodies of the afflicted people. It was said that people stuffed "posies," a type of flower, into their pockets so they couldn't smell the dead bodies that were piling up everywhere. The ashes fell after they began to burn the bodies so the infection could no longer spread. Although not everyone "fell down," The Black Death wiped out a significant 20% of the world's population. (Ryan, Ash)

CERN is "The European Organization for Nuclear Research" that operates the world's largest particle physics lab, and the LHC is an "atom smasher" to generate antimatter which is invisible. Because many are under Satan's authority, we can see that humans have become fascinated with trying to manipulate the circle of life. CERN is widely recognized as a circle and the facility houses the largest Hadron Collider, which is ALICE. ALICE stands for A Large Ion Collider Experiment. CERN scientists are in search of the god particle in which they believe will unveil the secrets of the universe. They believe that the universe is shaped like a cosmic tree." (Cern Accelerating Science) CERN scientists are really looking for the tree of life but will not find it, they will instead be led to death and destruction. They are seeking dark matter. This dark matter is the dark universe, also known as Satan himself.

In the grand scheme, the aim of CERN is to blast open a portal to admit demons to control the Earth. The Holy Spirit spoke to me through a dream saying that "the flood gates of hell are now open for the people to swiftly fall in." The Lord revealed this to me because He has said in His word that nothing will happen on this Earth that He will not forewarn his prophets of. There are claims that CERN scientists will make an announcement regarding a "new discovery" which is said to usher in a "New Golden Dawn." You may not be aware of this fact but The Hermetic Order of the Golden Dawn is a secret society devoted to the study and practice of the occult, metaphysics, and paranormal activities. (Hermetic Order of the Golden Dawn)

I want you to understand that COVID-19, the deaths, the vaccinations, the spazzing out of civilians, and the world chaos are not a coincidence. All of this has been planned out for decades. Prior to the government ever making an announcement regarding COVID-19 vaccinations, the Lord gave me a dream that would reveal the schemes of the devil. In the dream, I got in the car with my prayer partner. We were going to a particular nursing home to check on the sick and elderly just to volunteer for a few minutes. I got out of the car first. I saw a skinny older Black lady with grey hair. Her appearance was so fragile that the wind could have broken her. She was lying in her hospital bed.

I continued to walk to the main entrance. Then I saw a huge statue of a nurse holding the arm of another older Black woman. The nurse appeared to be dragging her by one arm. This older Black woman's eyes were widely stretched with red broken blood vessels in the shape of lighting. Her hair was gray and stringy. It stuck up on the top of her head and looked fried. It seemed everyone that came there was destined to die because the doctors and nurses were injecting the patients with some sort of slow-kill lethal injection. I stopped at the statue and the Holy Spirit said "pay attention to what's around you, even the grounds you sleep on because some grounds are cursed." I ran from the facility after seeing this. When I awoke I was troubled and prayed about it. A few weeks later, the vaccine was introduced worldwide. This is no coincidence because scientists have experimented for years with Blacks trying to find the God particle.

The goal of these people is to harness dark energy while in pursuit of the God particle and they are using God's people to do it. My prayer is that you understand the matrix that the elite of this world seeks to trap you in. They are responsible for the world wide web and predictive programming which is "Charlotte's Web." They want each person to be led down the rabbit hole known as the black hole. Do not become an experiment by rendering your vessels and minds over to the world of the occult.

I want to refer you to scripture which makes all of this plain. The name Abaddon or Apollyon appears in Revelation 9:11: "They had as king over them the angel of the Abyss," whose name in Hebrew is Abaddon, and in Greek, Apollyon. In Hebrew, the name "Abaddon" means a place of destruction. The Greek title "Apollyon" literally means "The Destroyer." In Revelation chapters 8 and 9, John describes a period during the end times when angels sound seven trumpets. Each trumpet signals the coming of a new judgment on the people of Earth. When the fifth angel blows his trumpet, the Abyss, a great smoking pit will open, and a horde of demonic locusts will rise out of it (Revelation 9:1-3). These creatures will be given the power to torture any person who does not bear God's seal. The pain they inflict will be so intense that sufferers will wish to die. This time is near people. You must break the curses over your life because again, each person who does not bear the seal of Christ will be tortured. The system as we know it will no longer be.

The information imparted to you is not intended to evoke fear in your heart, as fear is of Satan. But rather to set urgency about the coming of the Lord and the plagues that will consume all who don't break the curses and receive Jesus Christ as their personal Lord and savior. God's people should be courageous in this hour because we have been forewarned of what is to come. Sticking to God and having faith ensures our victory during calamity.

The black matter that the elite seek to harness is pushed through various agendas like the planned murder of Blacks worldwide. Every time you see a widely publicized story of an unjust killing of a Black man or woman it angers the Black community and evokes rage. Many protest in order to provoke change, not understanding that protesting will not help what has already been spiritually conceived. Most do not understand that chanting "Black Lives Matter'" is actually conjuring up the black matter occultists need. Most experts think that dark matter/black matter is abundant in the universe and that it has had a strong influence on its structure and evolution. (Dark Matter) This sounds identical to the influence Blacks have had as well. The chant "Black Lives Matter" said in unison by Black people sends vibrational energy into the universe as occultists have intended, to usher in their alleged "New Golden Dawn."

It is no coincidence that the world of the occult speaks esoterically to continuously deceive the general public into doing what these world leaders desire. Many elites study the Kabbalah and as part of their practice, they are well versed in Gematria. These elites control the media. Five or six corporations are the influences behind the media, they code their stories and sports with Gematria. It is no surprise that Black Lives Matter vibrates with crown chakra such as human souls are stars, author of destruction, an abomination of humanity, ending Golden Dawn, along with many other messages intended to be covered by using one phrase to summon other energies all with the same numerical values. What is portrayed is always a coded message and the further you understand it the more you're able to swiftly recognize what is really being said behind the headlines. They predict the future through these coded messages as well as raise energy to open the abyss. Black lives are being destroyed to attack the kingship originally placed inside of us, to use Black lives as blood sacrifices unto their gods in worldwide ritualistic ceremonies, and ultimately to make Blacks feel further oppressed as if we are an abomination to humanity.

Just like the passing down of tons of codes through Delta, this world at large operates off a coded system that only a select few understand, making them the elite while the others are just pawns in their game of chess. The goal is advancement but typically only the kings, queens, and royal players survive in the game. Hence the importance of returning to your birthright in Christ. When under the Satanic system of witchcraft, people tend to get entrapped further and further into the matrix without any real spiritual clarity and understanding. Protesting will not put a dent in the matrix, but renouncing the evil covenants, breaking the curses over your life, and turning from wicked involvement while seeking God to pour His spirit into you, will.

These evil-doers are committing treason against the sovereign people of God. It's spiritual warfare and it's manifesting itself physically. The world of light versus the world of darkness. God is sovereign. He gave us sovereignty. Satan gave us sorcery. We were meant to be free beings, never restricted and confined spiritually nor physically. Satan and his disciples are working through the elite of this world who have been in pursuit of kingship. They are aware that there's a time limit on the oppression and suppression of God's people and understand that their time is running out! Storms are being traded and a transfer is about to happen soon. The idea that God's people will be returning back to their original birthright frightens them. God is about to pour His spirit out upon His people so that their power will increase as no one has ever seen. I'm talking about a celestial power that will break the matrix system for the people of God. Those who bear God's seal will have protection over them making them more powerful than any man has ever seen. Scientists are working overtime to prevent this from happening. The only way they feel they can remain in control and have permanent rulership is to become immortal beings. In essence, become gods by manipulating the God particle found in the black matter and in Black people.

This is also the reason why there are more space launches than ever before and even more NASA products sold worldwide. The word NASA in Gematria has the same numerical code/vibration as "hidden code." Those who live under a curse oftentimes call prophecy a conspiracy. If you believe that what I am saying is far from the word of God I suggest you pick up your Bible and check your spiritual address. God instructs us to pay attention to the signs of the end times, not manipulate them. Whether you believe it or not, prophecies will come to pass. Elites' underground bunkers and established wealth will not save them. God has said in His word, "People will flee to caves in the rocks and to holes in the ground from the fearful presence of the LORD and the splendor of his majesty when He rises to shake the Earth." Isaiah 2:19.

Shifting back to when we were pyramids, if you recall, we were gathered in a dark sanctuary. Allow me to give you a breakdown of what was really taking place. The prophytes were in essence the false prophets leading us toward the "light." The candles were indicative of the false light of Satan, uniting the individual flames of each member to a unified flame orchestrated by the author of lies himself. White candles in Delta represent the fundamental principles of the sorority. In candle magic, the white candle also represents purity and innocence, spiritual enlightenment, cleansing, purification, peace, and truth. The red candle in Delta represents the torch of wisdom as the public motto for the organization is "intelligence is the torch of wisdom." In candle magic, the red candle represents the element of fire, love, power, strength, the blood of the moon, sexuality, and fast action in spell work. Lit candles have been known to help create a mystical and magical atmosphere during a ritual, especially in a dark atmosphere. They bring the element of fire and can be used to release or initiate something, hence we were in the first steps to initiation. The light of a candle also invites spirits.

Now having awareness of the magic I participated in and the altars that were erected unto Satan who was masked as Minerva, I discovered that Delta has blended ceremonial and elemental witchcraft. Elemental witches work their craft based on the four elements of water, fire, Earth, and air. This is heavily explored through the nine-day pathway during the initiation process. The aspects of rituals are utilized more than anything. Ceremonial witches invoke many different spiritual aspects in their ceremonial magic to assist them in their practice and in spell work. Light, sound, color, and vibrational energies are a part of evoking magical power in the world of witchcraft at large. In Delta's ritual book there is specific instruction on how to conduct each ceremony.

Exodus 20:24 reminds us that "An altar of earth thou shalt make unto me and shalt sacrifice thereon thy burnt offerings, and thy peace offerings, thy sheep, and thine oxen: in all places where I record my name I will come unto thee, and I will bless thee." In essence, God is setting forth the law of the altar and showing how He will bring blessings unto the altars erected unto Him yet the Satanic altars we knowingly or unknowingly bind ourselves to bring about curses. Spiritual law is spiritual law regardless if it is used in the kingdom of light or the kingdom of darkness.

Romans 6:16 says, "Do you not know that if you present yourselves to anyone as obedient slaves, you are slaves of the one whom you obey, either of sin, which leads to death, or of obedience, which leads to righteousness?" As much as it hurts to say this, I was an obedient slave to Satan through my membership with Delta, which led to destruction in my life. As pyramids, one of the first activities we learned was how to lock up. Standing in number order, in a straight line one behind the other. Our Dean of Pledges, also known as our "DP" or "Ma Duck," yelled out, "lock up!" In one fluent motion we would bind ourselves together. Locking up is a term used to describe an action that requires one pledgee to lock arms with another pledgee to form a chain link bounding the entire pledge class together. Looking back, it paralleled the way slaves were brought over from Africa on slave ships.

Ironically, when crossing over into Delta, the intake class is known as a line or ship. A ship name is chosen by the pledge class. The history of ship naming dates back to ancient Babylonian times. Mariners from Rome, Egypt, and Greece had also conducted christening ceremonies to seek help from their gods to protect their vessels before starting their first voyages. The ship names were typically the names of the Goddesses they worshipped and later after Queens and Princesses. Further proving the point that this entire world operates off rituals and ceremonies. (How Are Ships Named —Naming and Launching Ceremony) This type of watercraft is also the conduit of most witchcraft where the lines cross into the dark world via these Black Greek Letter organizations. The summoning of water spirits from the Marine kingdom is what their power is hinged upon.

Let's get back to locking up. After locking up we proceeded to perform what was called the "death march." Yes, the death march. With as much sense as we should have had, not one of us challenged this. It was something we all were awaiting the opportunity to do. A death march is a forced march of prisoners of war or other captives or deportees in which individuals are left to die along the way. Forced marches were utilized for slaves who were bought or captured by slave traders in Africa. (Death March) This same death march was the introduction to our new member presentation, which is commonly referred to as the coming-out show or probate show.

Probate courts administer the process by which the last will and testament of the deceased member are allocated according to what is written. Who would have ever known I would spiritually die and render my mind, body, and soul to Satan? The probate show was merely an outward presentation of Satan's slaves, dressed in red and black with masks covering our faces until the appropriate time. We sang praises to him through chants, gave reverence to the twenty-two founding members who made it possible for our new initiation into the dark world. Wow, what a wild road with Satan. 2 Peter 2:19 states, "They promise them freedom, but they themselves are slaves of corruption. For whatever overcomes a person, to that, he is enslaved."

At the time of crossing, members of the pledge class address one another as line sisters or LS. When one is referring to a member as a soror, they are essentially saying "star." When one says line sister they are unknowingly saying "align stars." In other words, the "stars aligning" refers to the astrological idea that when the positions of certain planets sit in defined angles (30 degrees, 90, 45, etc) in relation to the position they had at one's birth then good or bad things will happen. Hence why each member is given numbers. Additionally, prison inmates are given numbers to identify themselves, while Deltas are given line numbers and membership numbers as eternal slaves. After all, membership in the Delta organization is for a lifetime whether active or inactive.

There were great things that happened for many of the women I pledged with and women in chapters abroad, but my fate in Delta was the complete opposite. God was not pleased with the evil covenants I made in the dark and I would come to see the physical manifestation each and every day for nearly a decade. God's grace was sufficient. He understood my heart's desire to serve Him even while being under heavy witchcraft.

Thinking back to my pledge process, I can remember the night I got my line name vividly. We were in the woods as usual. It was a hot night. I was exhausted from the weeks of no sleep, constant thirst and hunger. I was pissed and over the process by then. It was finally my turn to be dubbed or renamed. It was time to transition from just a number to a name. My "special sister," who was always gracious to me, stood in front of me, made an invisible pyramid over my head as the rest of the big sisters chanted aloud "we dub thee," and said TASHA MAC. There are two sides to the name given.

I want to provide you with a quick backstory. Tasha Mack was a character during that time frame on a popular TV show called *The Game*. She was the mother and manager of the show's star quarterback Malik Wright. She grew up in Richmond, California, and had a baby in high school with her longtime boyfriend. Ultimately Tasha Mack was a strong Black woman but struggled in many aspects of her life from love, friendship, and even ended up losing her career.

Now let's get back to me being dubbed ... The special sister that was assigned to me said we gave you this name because you're like the single mother on your line. I immediately blurted out, "no I'm not," but was tapped by my line sister to hush before I got us all in trouble. She proceeded to say, "not in a bad way, it's just that you bear the weight of the world on your shoulders and take care of everybody's needs, neglecting yourself, but on a positive note, you're bold, charismatic, sassy, and you're into makeup." I rolled with it because I had no other choice, you don't choose your name, it's given. The name wasn't bad, but the meaning was terrible. Especially seeing as how in my own life I watched my mother struggle as a single mother my entire life. I had a moment of learning to accept my new name, but it was still a celebration for all of us. We were another step closer to finally becoming women of distinction. As a whole, we felt accomplished.

I informed you of how I became a victim of identity theft during my pledge process, that was a physical manifestation of what had already taken place spiritually. As humans, it is sometimes a challenge to understand a world we cannot see so we operate on a carnal level. Sure we've heard the statement as believers that "our weapons are not carnal," yet we still fight flesh and blood; not fully grasping the concept that there are unseen forces that operate the physical world we live in that are both good and evil. I stepped out of the will of God and pledged my allegiance to a deity under the authority of Satan. My desire to be amongst the elite of this world took me from my ultimate position of being the elect of God. This covenant put me under new orders and gave the evil forces legal jurisdiction to change my identity. My original birthright through the covenant God made with Abraham for his descendants was traded at the cost of joining the ranks of most prestigious and sophisticated women of the world. Talk about being bamboozled! Satan desires the youth more than anything primarily because of their naive mindset and moldability.

Satan tries to duplicate everything God does and uses subtle devices to deceive God's people into forming covenants that bind them to evil altars. He understands the importance of names. He himself was once Lucifer the archangel of music and when thrown out of heaven due to his pride, he was then renamed Satan, meaning adversary. Satan's pride and competition with his creator removed him from being God's servant to becoming God's direct adversary. Biblically, in Genesis 7:5-15 we see where God changed Abram's name, meaning "high father," to "Abraham," meaning "father of a multitude" and Abraham's wife's name from "Sarai," meaning "my princess," to "Sarah," meaning "mother of nations." He did this to transition them from one level to another and establish a new covenant. Just as my name through Delta had been changed to establish a new identity and a new covenant.

What one envisions to be a dream come true could actually be an entrapment by the enemy. This is much deeper than most care to give awareness to. In hindsight, I had no idea I was changing the course of my life for the worst. Especially because from the outside looking in, this was everything I wanted and more. On top of that, this was something that I loved and enjoyed, despite the obstacles. I share all of this to let you know that I lived my life in a curse I was not even aware of being in. The beginning of living in a curse can seem like bliss because of one's ignorance, but before long it will become tortuous and dark.

We're taught in Delta that intelligence is the torch of wisdom. However, the law of God states the fear of the Lord is the beginning of all wisdom. Jesus is the Light. A torch doesn't compare to the light of Christ. Crossing the burning sands in the Greek world was equivalent to Moses parting the Red Sea to help God's people cross over from the house of bondage in Egypt where the Egyptians worshiped Pagan gods. Unfortunately, when crossing over in Delta, I went back into bondage serving Pagan gods and reversing God's original will. Crossing the burning sands is an important ritual in the Greek world. The term "crossing the burning sands" describes pledging a Greek-letter organization and crossing over from being a pledge to becoming a full member. Satan duplicates everything, he uses fire and God uses water in the following examples. This leads us to baptism. In John 3:5 Jesus answered, "Truly, truly, I say to you, unless one is born of water and the Spirit, he cannot enter the kingdom of God."

The only way you can become a full member in Delta is after crossing the burning sands. Mark 16:16 reads, "Whoever believes and is baptized will be saved, but whoever does not believe will be condemned." Lastly,

Matthew 28:19 states, "Go therefore and make disciples of all nations, baptizing them in the name of the Father and of the Son and of the Holy Spirit," Jesus commanded his disciples to go to all nations and baptize them with water in the name of the Father and of the Son and of the Holy Spirit. He sent them out two by two. At my crossing-over ceremony, my line sisters and I went two by two reciting the various components and forwarding through the ritual until we all completed the pathway. Our exact time was recorded and kept sacred by the keeper of muses and graces. Isn't it ironic that the names muses and graces are similar to grace and mercy? Satan sends his disciples out who in Delta return as big sisters to pledge and cross others over the burning sands.

Many will still argue that this organization does not serve another god, so then why is there a position in the organization called "The keeper of Muses and Graces?" Let's take a further look at Muses. Muses are an ancient Greek religion and mythology. The Muses are the inspirational goddesses of literature, science, and the arts. They were considered the source of the knowledge embodied in the poetry, lyric songs, and myths that were related orally for centuries in ancient Greek culture. (Muses) In my research, I've found that there are nine muses, which I had no idea of during my involvement with Delta. I can't help but think that there are nine cardinal virtues in Delta. In Greek mythology, a Charis pronounced or Grace is one of three or more goddesses of charm, beauty, nature, human creativity, goodwill, and fertility. Together they are known as the Charites or Graces. The cult of the Charites is very old. (Charis Name) All of this showcases the Pagan worship I partook of while in the world of the occult.

Satan's goal is to deceive God's people by using likened things. God gave us "Grace and Mercy" not "Muses and Graces." Grace is the help given to us by God because God desires us to have it, not necessarily because of anything we have done to earn it. Ephesians 2:8-9 says, "For by grace you have been saved through faith. And this is not your own doing; it is the gift of God, not a result of works, so that no one may boast."

Some would question, how could the members of such organizations not know the full capacity of what they decided to join? Simply put, it's the smoke and mirrors effect. The truth was embellished with misleading information, it was all an illusion. Most people can understand being in a relationship with someone, truly loving them, and being willing to do anything for them. During the relationship, you dismiss the obvious signs allowing love to cover a multitude of faults only to end up finding that what you thought was love was a figment of your imagination and that is where the rubber hits the road. It's easy to be deceived when you can only see the good in something. The Bible says in Matthew 24:24 that even the elect will be deceived if that is at all possible by the great signs and wonders of the false prophets.

A common misconception is that these groups are as gruesome as some movies try to portray. Because they are secret societies, the absence of information leads people to believe the worst. I was never beaten, made to sleep with men or do crazy things in the graveyards, etc. I can't speak for anybody else but I am speaking from my experience. Those are things I would have easily walked away from. The devil is cunning and gets you in ways you can't identify in your ignorance. As the king of pride and author of lies, his trickery is top-notch, make no mistake about it.

I am not singling out this particular organization as a means to bash its members because I was one and devoted a large portion of my life to serving alongside these women. I have called them sister, soror, mentor, and family. But what I have been commanded to do is to use my experience and newfound enlightenment to expose the schemes by the elite, which have deceived the elect of God. Can I speak fully about any other organization? No because I have never pledged to them, but what I can do is speak in love and truth from a journey I have walked back and forth.

As I mentioned before, a woman from an entirely different Divine 9 organization shed light on the Pagan worship behind all of the organizations. Members of these Black Greek Organizations will oppose what I have to say by arguing that each organization is different as is each chapter.

But one should understand that every organization has a standardized intake process for its new initiates that are coupled with rituals and ceremonies to ensure that members worldwide share some of the same experiences. Moreover, each organization has a patron that is worshipped through song, prayers, etc. The patron, colors, and names of organizations for sororities, fraternities, masons, eastern stars, etc. may differ but they are all powered by Satan. The use of biblical scriptures throughout various rituals makes it hard to believe that one is engaging in anything other than that of Christ. On top of that, the actual great works done abroad are without a doubt beneficial to all recipients.

Undoubtedly, the women of Delta are powerful beings who have committed their lives to serve in their communities and provoke change. They are world leaders, mentors, and were once the type of woman I wanted to become, so I did. I didn't join the group for friends or popularity. I joined for the opportunity to serve and advance my life in every way. But as the Bible teaches, "what does it profit a man to gain the world but to lose his soul?" All of the great works done mean nothing because each person who has committed their life to any god other than Christ Jesus will lift their eyes in hell according to the laws of God. Non-believers who are not striving to spend eternity with Jesus Christ can disregard this entire book, but people who claim to serve the one and true living God should decide on where they stand. "I call heaven and earth as witnesses today against you, that I have set before you life and death, blessing and cursing; therefore choose life, that both you and your descendants may live;" Deuteronomy 30:19

3

"Revelation from God."
THE SPIRIT OF SHIANDA #5

The Spirit of Shianda was the spirit assigned to my life when I affirmed the oath to Delta and this spirit housed a legion of demons. Just as God has assigned angels to us, Satan has also assigned demons to wage war against our destinies. The Spirit of Shianda was specifically assigned to block and hinder every blessing the Lord originally ordained for my life. This spirit was sent to ensure I fell victim to non-marriage, single motherhood, a struggling career, financial lack, and physical deterioration. The Spirit of Shianda attacked every God-given gift. This revelation from God about the Spirit of Shianda was the turning point in my life. The more information God downloaded in my spirit the more I craved the understanding of God. It's hard to fix a problem when you don't understand the root cause of it.

I was confused at first because I could not find anything in scripture about this demonic force, but then I was led to an account in the Bible that gave further revelation about what I was dealing with. Just as angels have names so do demons and that is evident in Mark 5:"Then they came to the other side of the sea, to the country of the Gadarenes. And when He had come out of the boat, immediately there met Him out of the tombs, a man with an unclean spirit, who had *his* dwelling among the tombs; and no one could bind him, not even with chains, because he had often been bound with shackles and chains. And the chains had been pulled apart by him, and the shackles broken in pieces; neither could anyone tame him. And always, night and day, he was in the mountains and in the tombs, crying out and cutting himself with stones. When he saw Jesus from afar, he ran and worshiped Him. And he cried out with a loud voice and said, 'What have I to do with You, Jesus, Son of the Most High God? I implore You by God that You do not torment me.' For He said to him, 'Come out of the man, unclean spirit!' Then He asked him, 'What *is* your name?' And he answered, saying, 'My name *is* Legion; for we are many.'"

When Jesus cast out the demons they went into a herd of about two thousand pigs. The demonic spirit caused the pigs to rush down the hill and drown. Do you see how one demon-possessed man could house thousands of spirits which caused him to act in an inhumane way? He was being controlled by unseen forces that were not himself and were of course far from the spirit of God. These legions of demons were no match to the power of God, but it was only through the authority of Jesus could the demons be cast out. That scripture illustrates how spirits can cause you to suffer in every aspect of your life. Some folks have a tendency to downplay just how strong demonic forces really are. Demons are not fictional but rather powerful entities with names and can be erected from altars all over the Earth.

The Spirit of Shianda desired to break the spirit of God within me, causing me to become a slave to Satan while he ruled as my master. My mind became programmed to believe that I was weak where I was once strong. The Spirit of Shianda bound me to a legion of demonic spirits.

THE SPIRIT OF POVERTY:

The spirit of poverty frustrates and stops you from earning money, ensures that the resources you need are stolen, unsearchable or delayed, will make you work until the point of painful exhaustion while receiving little to nothing for your labor. It even causes you to make mistakes, poor decisions, and experience forgetfulness. The little that you have always depletes quickly and secretly. The Bible reminds us that Satan plucks up every good seed planted. This diabolic spirit can show itself in many ways: spiritually where one can never gain true revelation through Christ, mentally where one lacks memorization and general understanding, physically where a person faces chronic illness and seems to never achieve stability, and financially where the lack of money prevents you from living a good quality life, as well as a lack of accomplishments and a continuous cycle of poor relationships. This only adds frustration to your life, not value. As you can see, poverty is not just financial but can show itself as an impoverished state of being.

The love of money is the root of all kinds of evil but access to it can solve many problems. In order to fulfill our assignments, it takes resources to get them done. God's perfect will is outlined in the 3rd book of John 1:2, "Beloved, I pray that you may prosper in all things and be in health, just as your soul prospers." That reassures me that God never intended for there to be lack in my life of any type. Biblically, we can see several accounts of where poverty of all sorts was a curse, due to the disobedience of God's people. In Deuteronomy 28, God speaks of the blessings He has in store for those who obey Him but subsequently reveals the course of life for those who disobey Him.

Let's examine verses 15 through 28, "But if you will not obey the voice of the Lord your God or be careful to do all his commandments and his statutes that I command you today, then all these curses shall come upon you and overtake you. Cursed shall you be in the city, and cursed shall you be in the field. Cursed shall be your basket and your kneading bowl. Cursed shall be the fruit of your womb and the fruit of your ground, the increase of your herds and the young of your flock. Cursed shall you be when you come in, and cursed shall you be when you go out." "The Lord will send on you curses, confusion, and frustration in all that you undertake to do until you are destroyed and perish quickly on account of the evil of your deeds because you have forsaken me. The Lord will make the pestilence stick to you until he has consumed you off the land that you are entering to take possession of it. The Lord will strike you with wasting disease and with fever, inflammation, and fiery heat, and with drought and with blight and with mildew. They shall pursue you until you perish. And the heavens over your head shall be bronze, and the earth under you shall be iron. The Lord will make the rain of your land powder. From heaven, dust shall come down on you until you are destroyed."

If people are not convinced that God is real and that as He blesses, He will also curse according to one's disobedience, I could only hope that sharing my story will make someone a believer. Although I blindly and innocently partook in Satanic rituals, I was still guilty according to the law of God. As with the laws of the land, ignorance of the law is no excuse.

While the spirit of poverty overtook my life there was rejection from all angles. I had once been a person where acceptance was the norm but now there was rejection. I could be in the grocery store and get the nastiest attitudes from workers when asking a question or checking out. The same thing happened on jobs. I was once employed by a woman whom I revered and it seemed like before long I was pestered about things that didn't make sense. She made it clear that there was not enough room for us both there. The environment became uncomfortable and she gave me an ultimatum that would force me out of the situation since her desire was to control my every move. On another job, there was a young lady who would always abandon her shift. She lied to the owner of the company and I was fired unjustly that day. Whenever I undertake a position I do my very best so my work ethic speaks volumes. I was never late, called off from work, or took a sick day but I was still fired. The managers never had any complaints, in fact, they were always impressed. This goes to show that Satan will do whatever he pleases to you when you are under his authority. He is the author of confusion. They never gave me an explanation as to why they fired me but called three days later to offer me a promotion at a downgraded facility. Higher pay was offered to undertake a more stressful workload. It didn't make sense because no one would fire you then call you back to promote you. I'm sure they understood the major loss they would experience after my termination. Satan drives people to reject what benefits them out of pride but in their quiet time, they question their poor decisions. I denied their offer. There was no way I would continue to render services to anyone who would blatantly disrespect my hardwork and commitment for a non-credible source.

These are the types of strange things that were happening for years to me, being framed to be something I wasn't. I was accused of being the problem but no one could ever present substantial evidence to prove their lies. All of these situations were beginning to beat me down. I felt like people saw me as a punching bag and took their jab whenever they pleased. The most hurtful part for me was getting evil in exchange for kindness. If I punched someone in the face and they punched me back I would understand that. But here it is you're in your lane trying to sort out life and out of nowhere someone comes and punches you for no reason. It is not just physically painful but mentally antagonizing.

Many people will paint you out to be problematic when facing trouble on every hand much like they did Job in the Bible. Another biblical account of unjust treatment is shown through Joseph. Joseph was an excellent servant to Potiphar but Potiphar's wife lied concerning Joseph. She accused him of attempted rape after Joseph denied her sexual advancements. Potiphar's wife was the evil one but Joseph was thrown in prison for a lie. You must understand what I did not understand during those times. The spirits that work within these people understand that when the curses are broken over your life, your light will be untamable. They know this and seek to keep you oppressed spiritually, mentally, physically, and financially. These accounts are not normal and indicate witchcraft activities in your life. The Spirit of Shianda was working overtime to alter my destiny. I would later be hit soul-deep when experiencing total chaos and confusion in ministry.

THE SPIRIT OF LEVIATHAN:

So many of us are ignorant to the spirits that wage war against us in our personal lives, on our jobs, and even in ministry. The Spirit of Shianda also summoned the spirit of Leviathan. The Leviathan Spirit has many characteristics, but it mainly manifests itself as pride. The very word "Leviathan" means "to twist." Leviathan is often given the physical attributes of a giant serpent-like sea creature. According to Strong's Concordance, Leviathan is depicted as "a wreathed animal or serpent," just like in the laurel wreath of Minerva, no coincidence there but I digress. Similarly, Leviathan is a water spirit from the marine kingdom. The most detailed description of Leviathan can be found in the 41st chapter of the book of Job, in which God asks Job if he can handle a battle with this apparently unbeatable monster. Leviathan is described as exhaling smoke and having scales, breath like hot coals, and sharp teeth that are "terrible roundabout." The spirit of Leviathan attacks believers by causing them to turn away from God. I can attest to this as I was seriously considering delving fully into manifesting the life I wanted through divination.

The physical depiction of Leviathan as a powerful serpent can also be seen as symbolizing a spiritual monster that wants to squeeze the spirit of Christ out of Christian believers in the same way a python squeezes the life out of its prey. As a result, actual physical pain and infirmities are associated with Leviathan. Physical manifestations of the Leviathan spirit include pain and stiffness in the neck and shoulder area. For two years straight I suffered from a frozen shoulder that sprang up out of nowhere. I went to sleep one night and woke up with restricted use of my shoulder. I struggled with basic daily activities like fastening my bra, fully extending my arm, exercising, etc. It was truly a painful process. No therapy helped neither did prescribed medications. Prayer and fasting caused that spirit to be released. That is when I gained full use and mobility of my arm again. Leviathan is also known to be responsible for a dream in which you feel your breathing is constricted and you are being choked. I experienced a series of torturous dreams as such.

Speaking of dreams, I had a vivid dream of being on a ship that was being steered out of control by a man I was unfamiliar with. His wife pleaded with him to slow down. She wanted him to stop his reckless behavior; however he did not take heed to her plea. The man was careless and endangered the lives of the other passengers on board including myself. I was ejected from the ship and landed under the sea. I saw huge species in the marine kingdom. What I did not know is that God was showing me the pending attack of these water spirits. God revealed later that the octopus I saw was a spirit of mind control, there were many elements of the dream that paralleled what would later happen in ministry. Satan tried his best to turn me away from God even in the very place where I opened my spirit to God.

Leviathan levied his heaviest attack in the ministry I was a part of. During this time I was seeking spiritual refuge amidst my car repossession and homelessness. I spent countless hours in church and doing ministry-related activities. The Leviathan spirit operates by causing division through twisting communication, accusations, misunderstandings, and utter chaos. This all leads to quarrels, separation, and isolation. It twists the meaning of words and seeks to destroy the unity of people. It finds a willing spirit and operates through the individual causing everyone to turn against you. It seeks to divide and dismember the relationships God has connected you to in the body of Christ. It perpetuates accusations against you, and this is exactly what took place. What started out as a loving ministry quickly flipped. The spirit of jealousy took root and I was accused of some of the most diabolical things. No one understood my struggle or empathized with what I was going through. I was at my lowest and kicked while I was down.

The Spirit of Leviathan twisted every action, every gesture, and every good thing into evil. The Bible says, "Woe unto them that call evil good, and good evil; that put darkness for light, and light for darkness; that put bitter for sweet, and sweet for bitter!" What I came to deal with was disgusting. I did not expect things to take a turn for the worst but God prophesied the end early on. Can you see the pattern? There is always a liar that Satan uses to falsely accuse a just person in an attempt to kill their good reputation. In the Bible, Satan used Potiphar's self-seeking, lustful, manipulative wife, and in ministry, Satan will often use people who suffer from some of the same spirits to try to get those that love you to hate you. Potiphar's wife could not have her way with Joseph so she lied to get her way.

The spirits of pride, jealousy, and envy drive many who hold seats and positions in the household of faith to do some of the most ungodly things. I viewed this at the time as a setback, but God was setting me up for a great promotion just as He did with Joseph. I don't care what anybody tells you, church hurt is real. We render time in exchange for money at a job but in ministry, we open our spirit in exchange for the love and peace of God. When you're in ministry and God tells you to be quiet amidst the hurt, that's when it feels like you've been gut-punched. It truly is a humbling experience. Typically in the world you do and say what you will, but in church you try to be respectful. You can't get some things off your chest, especially not in the manner you may desire. That burning anger can only be comforted by God and true justice. To be attacked by Satan and his minions is a whole nother level of hurt while in the household of faith. The household of faith eventually felt like a slaughterhouse and God was ushering me out.

THE NUMBER 5:

If you recall in the previous passages, when the Spirit of Shianda was initially spoken of to me by the Holy Spirit in my dream, the number five also appeared. I began thinking of the number and where it had appeared in my life. After the revelation by God of the Spirit of Shianda and its negative effects, I took to my affiliation with the occult to see what I'd find. The 5th jewel of Delta Sigma Theta Sorority, Incorporated is fidelity. I realized that my steadfast devotion, loyalty, and commitment to the organization upon initiation was something that was hindering me in my spiritual walk with God and in my life's progress. Although I was proclaiming the name of the Lord with my mouth, my spirit was bound to the Satanic altar that was erected that Spring when I took the oath and made the pledge of my life even until death to another god. Matthew 6:24 states that "No man can serve two masters: for either he will hate the one, and love the other; or else he will hold to the one, and despise the other. Ye cannot serve God and mammon." Neither can one serve God and Minerva or whatever has served as an idol above God in your life.

The organization has a five-point programmatic thrust, one being international awareness and involvement. During my tenure in the organization, I learned of the many efforts by the organization to expand the "Mary Help of the Sick Mission Hospital" in Thika, Kenya. I had a great interest to serve there with fellow members internationally. The facility happens to be roughly eight hours from a town called Shianda. According to the Western Focus Community Organization (WEFOCO), Shianda consists of around 100,000 people and is very impoverished compared to the other places in Western Kenya. The area has a high population of individuals infected with HIV and AIDS, which leads to a high number of orphans and vulnerable children. There is a high poverty level due to unemployment, low job opportunities, lack of education, and poor agricultural farming methods. Drug abuse, crime, young girls resulting to commercial sex work, and gender inequality are all societal issues in this land. This further confirmed the revelation God showed me regarding the Spirit of Shianda. A spirit that was named after a poverty-stricken, infested land had polluted my life and destiny. Prior to God revealing the spirit I had no knowledge that Shianda, Kenya even existed.

Delta has a Five-Point Thrust while a largely recognized symbol in the occult is the five-point star. The five-point star is the pentagram. There are five pyramids in a pentagram. "Pentagrams were used symbolically in ancient Greece and Babylonia. They are used today as a symbol of faith by many Wiccans, akin to the use of the cross by Christians." *(Pentagram)* The pentagram is also used as a symbol by other belief systems and is associated with Freemasonry.

Satanist Aleister Crowley also made use of the pentagram in his Thelemic system of magic. The pentagram was used in ancient times as a Christian symbol for the five senses or of the five wounds of Christ. Anything used by Christians, Satan typically perverts its meaning.

Occult members believe in this mantra: "Let us keep the figure of the Five-pointed Star always upright, with the topmost triangle pointing to heaven, for it is the seat of wisdom, and if the figure is reversed, perversion and evil will be the result." *(Bard)* Obviously Delta's official symbol is a pyramid but that also reminded me of the tradition of collecting twenty-two elephants with their trunks up as members of Delta. That tradition came about with the passing of Florence Letcher Toms, a founding member of Delta Sigma Theta Sorority Incorporated. When she passed away her collection of elephants was donated to the Grand Chapter of Delta Sigma Theta Sorority, Incorporated, where they are on display in their archives at Delta's National Headquarters. Today most Deltas collect elephants in her honor. The elephant symbolizes strength and determination. We were told the uplifted trunk represents high goals but it definitely has more meaning than just that. Elephants are the largest animal in the world and they communicate through vibrations.

The world of the occult communicates esoterically. "Esoteric most commonly means obscure and only understood or intended to be understood by a small number of people with special and perhaps secret knowledge. It's often used to describe knowledge that's only intended to be revealed to people who have been initiated into a certain group." *(Esoteric Definition & Meaning)* God is a God of numbers and that is evident in the Bible so Satan emulates that. The world of the occult communicates esoterically through numbers, colors, light, and sound. Esoteric Science teaches that every sound in the visible world awakens its corresponding sound in the invisible realms, and arouses to action some force or other on the occult side of nature. Remember they operate off of vibrational energy. Moreover, in their world, every sound corresponds to a color and a number and to a sensation on some plane.

That can also be seen in the chakra chart. The very sound made in Delta summons spirits from the Satanic Kingdom. When spelled out, the sound made has five letters. The unofficial call made by members of Delta is OO-OOP. As I researched more about Greek customs I found that the word Opa parallels the call we made after being initiated as members. The Greeks use this as a call for attention, an invitation to join in a circle dance or a cry as the flame is lit. It has been known to invite "good spirits." According to an article by deTraci Regula of ThoughtCo, The actual meaning of "Opa!" is more like "Oops" or "Whoops!" Among Greeks, you might hear it after someone bumps into something or drops or breaks an object. Much like the breaking of plates in Greek restaurants and nightclubs as a sound of praise for the singers, dancers, or other performers. (*Greek Word for Satisfaction*) I found it no coincidence that we sounded off the call to get the attention of other Sorors, make our presence known in a large arena, or during strolls and steps in support of fellow sorority members. Again, we were only graced with the privilege after having crossed into the organization. We were broken into a different world.

The Bible states in 1 Corinthians 15:52, "In a moment, in the twinkling of an eye, at the last trumpet. For the trumpet will sound, and the dead will be raised imperishable, and we shall be changed." Satan uses what is pure for evil. The elephant makes a trumpet sound and the members of Delta use that energy to send an alert out. Every time I sounded that call, I was summoning spirits unknowingly. Shamans and Lightworkers have been known to use elephants as spirit guides. (*Elephant Symbolism & Meaning: SPIRIT, Totem, & Power Animal*) Elephants are pregnant for twenty-two months, there are twenty-two founders and the number twenty-two is also associated with the new world order.

Keeping with my evaluation of the number 5, God was revealing that this spirit toiled with my mind and attacked all five of my senses, my sight, touch, taste, smell, and hearing. "The organs associated with each sense sends information to the brain to help us transmit information." (*Bradford*) The presence of witchcraft of any sort in our lives skews our abilities physically and spiritually. Jesus knew how important these senses were. This is why He healed. Our senses help us to connect spiritually.

"The blind receive their sight, and the lame walk, the lepers are cleansed, and the deaf hears, the dead are raised up, and the poor have the gospel preached to them," Matthew 11:5. According to Bible scholars, the number 5 signifies the impotence of man. Man's helplessness is the reason for God's grace and favor. Man has no power of his own and cannot prosper except when God has willed it. I appreciated discovering this and more so for God choosing to reveal His desire to bring me out of darkness into His marvelous light by His grace and mercy.

The fifth book of the Bible is Deuteronomy where it outlines the laws for the children of Israel to keep them from offending God. This book is also rich in the promises God ordained for those who obey Him. The birthright of the children of God was to be blessed in our going out and in our coming in as it states in Deuteronomy 28. However, Satan comes to kill, steal, and destroy especially when you have been picked by God as His elect. Satan is jealous and wishes that the lives of those who love the Lord come to waste.

Lastly, the Lord's Tabernacle in the Wilderness holds strong spiritual significance and reflects God's grace with the use of the number five in the Old Testament. It was literally the house of God on Earth. This tabernacle, whose design was given directly by God, contained five curtains (Exodus 26:3), five bars (Exodus 26:26 —27), five pillars, and five sockets (Exodus 26:37), and an altar made of wood that was five cubits long and five cubits wide (Exodus 27:1). The height of the court within the tabernacle was five cubits (Exodus 27:18).

Through divine impartation, God was aiding me in destroying the evil covenants so that I could become a new creature in Him. As a member of the body, I had a function that I could not fully perform because I was spiritually paralyzed. Symbolically, we are the church and should be carrying out our roles for Christ. Through the knowledge of Christ and the implementation of His laws, I gained my liberty.

4

"I'M GOING TO CHURCH BUT NOT GROWING."
INFORMATION WITHOUT APPLICATION IS USELESS

Growing up in a Pentecostal church, I was taught to never question God because He is all-seeing and all-knowing and we should never question the works of the King. That's garbage, in my opinion. Not to bash the church or the people who claim to know God, but it is that very same mindset and misguidance that kept me in spiritual and physical bondage for years. Unfortunately, we continue to pass on diabolic ideologies until someone who receives divine impartation decides to break the cycle. The truth is, if you read the word of God for yourself, you'll see where the men and women of God had open dialogues with the Lord. King David had such a beautiful relationship with God that he asked Him questions regularly about the moves he should make as they related to life and war.

Cursing God and seeking clarity takes on two very different connotations. Religion teaches us not to bother Jesus. A real relationship with God will bring about divine revelation to the things plaguing your mind. Here is why you should question God: because He is your Father and wants to have a relationship with you. When we do things without having the understanding for ourselves, they never yield profitable endings. Much of what we blame God for is not Him at all. Some battles are fiery attacks of the enemy. To be real with you, I was in church but was ignorant of the laws of God. Of course I knew the basics like don't have sex before marriage, don't lie, steal, cheat, you know the cookie-cutter stuff that makes you feel like a good person if you adhere to it. Unfortunately, I had been given a great deal of information without any application for myself. Let me paint a picture for you of what that looks like: imagine a person who can repeat scriptures from head knowledge but has no idea how to activate the laws of God spiritually. You're probably thinking, what a waste, and you're right, it is. When taught that questioning something makes you defiant, it is easy to walk through life accepting what is presented instead of challenging ideas and concepts that you don't fully understand.

Many of us have known God through someone else as opposed to knowing Him for ourselves. I can't begin to explain how debilitating that is. Because I did not know God for myself, I fell into traps of deception when I went off to college. I was blind as a young adult, walking through life with my spiritual eyes wide shut. I had no real discernment. I was unprepared to step into the next phase of my life. I was about to enter into a spiritual battle that I had no idea about, taking all the shots because I had no armor or weapons. I was living life without understanding God's laws. Unaware, I became in breach. There are consequences when you break the law. As we know, ignorance of the law is no excuse. Many churches we have attended for years introduced us to manipulation through religious traditions as opposed to inviting true freedom through creating a personal relationship with our creator. Instead of preaching about wardrobe, I wish someone would have equipped me for warfare and exposed me to the schemes of the devil. While going to church, I failed to get an understanding of God and His adversary, Satan. I was taught to keep the laws of man instead of the laws of God. "My people perish for a lack of knowledge," Hosea 4:6. "But through knowledge the just shall be delivered," Proverbs 11:9.

5

"You can't wear the cloak of clergy and the cloak of curses at the same time. Pick a side. Choose life or death"
THE CLOAK OF CURSES

Church members, bishops, apostles, pastors, prophets, and prophetesses are wearing the cloak of the clergy as well as the cloak of curses. They are carrying their Bibles as well as their ritual books, not understanding that you cannot serve two masters or lead God's people while doing so. God would not allow me to lead His people while being under the headship of Satan. The Bible teaches that whatever flows from the head will trickle down to the beard. In layman's terms that means whatever authority the leaders are under, so too is the congregation.

    I have heard many varying viewpoints of men and women who are leaders in the body of Christ as well as Greek affiliated. The top one is, "my Greek affiliation has not turned me from God but rather has allowed me to use my influence to bring others to the kingdom." This is a situation that must be addressed because being in a position of power while convincing others that they can serve other gods will lead the masses to hell. Serving people in the community does not justify serving another god. It is idolatry, which is an abomination and is an excuse for staying in sin. Let's be real, you can serve the community and God at the same time, there's no need for Greek affiliations to accomplish that goal.

THE SPIRIT OF SHIANDA

Worshipping God in spirit and truth would mean we don't need letters, colors, calls, strolls, or steps to magnify the name of the Lord. No, we don't have to stay confined to a church setting. We should go out and be witnesses for the kingdom. The trick of the devil is to place you in an arena to do good things but not God things. As a former member of a Black Greek Letter Organization, I can identify with the level of pride one takes in their allegiance to their sorority/fraternity. One admirable aspect that I appreciated about Greek life is that the members are very disciplined and orderly when it comes to business. In that world everything is sacred. The candle placement, the lighting during ceremonies, and the spirit can only be ushered in a particular way which is outlined in the ritual book. I have never in my life been a part of anything as orderly. These women do everything with excellence.

Here is where the church failed. Most churches collectively have become lazy, self-centered, and their members seem dead. On the other hand, these Greek organizations are well organized and top tier when it comes to handling business. The level of structure is mind-blowing. The members of these groups lead with excitement and their zeal for life is contagious. I've personally witnessed Greek organizations give more to communities than churches. I have seen many churches take from people more than they open their hands to serve.

As a young adult wanting more out of life, your average churchgoer doesn't seem to be the goal. Instead, people who are well connected, well-rounded, have fun, travel, do great things, and work with people for a common goal are the ones I and many other people I knew wanted to follow. They know how to create disciples. If the people of God understood this concept there would be more people that would stay on the path of righteousness. Before I became a Delta I was intrigued by the members. My point is, I don't know many Christians who are non-Greek affiliated living a life worth following and that is a problem. Christ Himself was intriguing enough to draw a crowd and captivate the masses. No one wants to follow robotic people.

Today it seems like joining churches takes your personality away through the traditions that must be upheld, and that is not what God intended. Meanwhile, Greek organizations give you a platform to develop your gifts and talents. These organizations sharpen your skills and polish you through training, mentoring, etc. They understand how to breed quality people. This is what we should be doing in the body of Christ. People should not have to look outside for what should be taught in the house of God. There are not many inner-city schools you can go to and not see Greek-affiliated teachers, principals, etc. as the leaders. Having a primary focus on the Black community, these members understand the importance of elevating the next generation.

By experience, most of my favorite teachers were Greeks, women of Delta to be exact. These women took time to groom me. They prepared me for scholarship interviews, took me through formal etiquette training, and taught me what it meant to distinguish myself amongst the pact. This is something my church could not do because its members had never gone where I was intended to go as it related to success or spiritually in Christ.

People are going to church and not being blessed, many are poverty-stricken and sickly. To be honest, that in itself turns adults from wanting to be a part of ministries as such. People do not want to stay in negative environments or in places where they feel they are not growing. This is a generation interested in growing, not just showing up to socialize. Churches question why membership retention is not there and that is why. There's more judgment and traditions than teaching the truth with practical application. In the world of the occult, they are very goal-oriented and help their members see results. Think about it, no one hires a personal trainer not to see results, there is an expectation. In the same way, a baby will not continue to latch onto its mother's breast if she is not producing milk. I've witnessed more theatrics than result-based programming to elevate the people of God in ministry. There are a few churches that focus on this aspect and for those that do, I pray that God continues to keep His hand upon those ministries.

Understand that some who join these Greek organizations do not have a goal to rebel against God. They are determined to prosper because God placed a will to succeed inside of them and are cleaving to a source that ensures success. Satan understands that and uses his trickery to deceive innocent people into serving him for temporary gain and worldly fame. I've always wondered, if God is a God of plenty, then why do the real people of God seem to have so little? A lack of knowledge and generational curses are the reasons. Many churches have information but no spiritual understanding. If more of God's people understood the traps that are set by Satan, I believe that many of the wrong turns could be avoided altogether.

God never intended for us to be entangled in a cloak of curses but instead to wear a robe of righteousness. Isaiah 61:10 states, "I will greatly rejoice in the Lord; my soul shall exult in my God, for He has clothed me with the garments of salvation; He has covered me with the robe of righteousness, as a bridegroom decks himself like a priest with a beautiful headdress, and as a bride adorns herself with her jewels." God planned to prosper us and not harm us, but when we choose not to be cleansed through the blood of Jesus Christ and to remove the cloak of iniquity, we'll continuously offend our Father and miss the kingdom of heaven. It is important for all to understand, if you are a member of a Greek affiliated organization, Masonry, or Eastern Stars, you are in the world of the occult under the ordinance of Satan and out of the will of God. You cannot serve two masters. It doesn't matter how much one says they serve Jesus Christ. When you take an oath and pledge your allegiance to an organization it is not unto Christ. The papers were signed, the oath was affirmed and you are bound to the altar evoked at the time of your initiation until you spiritually and physically renounce your affiliation.

When I found out the truth behind these organizations I wanted out immediately because I desired for my soul to be saved above anything. In sharing my testimony some Greeks have sarcastically made comments stating, "I'm sorry for your experience," when in reality I'm sorry for their ignorance. God's people perish for a lack of knowledge but reject the truth when the lie benefits them. Unfortunately, many will go to the grave serving another god while claiming Christ. We get one life and there are no do-overs. If you choose to stay in, then you have chosen death. If you choose to renounce, then you have chosen life. Either way, your decision does not just affect you but your lineage as well up to the third and fourth generation according to Exodus 34:7.

"Let God be true, and every man a liar."
—Romans 3:4

6

"The elect of God has been deceived by the elite of this world."
STOLEN IDENTITY

It is a part of us as humans to feel a sense of belonging, it makes us feel secure as a people. For many Black people, so much of our culture has been stripped from us that it is hard to find our place and the path that leads to fulfillment. When you don't understand who you are and whose you are, you'll find yourself connecting with people and things that seemingly fill the void in that unfulfilled space. The quest to self-discovery and belongingness oftentimes leads to a path entangled in a whirlwind of curses. We search in all the wrong places, which pushes us further from Christ. We then find ourselves joining organizations that display "Black Excellence" and most of the time are Greek affiliated, as this is the only image of greatness many Blacks can identify with. Our heroes are local church leaders, teachers, doctors, entertainers, athletes, and community leaders, and we tend to follow in their footsteps as opposed to following God. Truth is, many of us don't identify with how Jesus is commonly depicted —" blonde-haired, blue-eyed" hanging on a cross, and because of this many Blacks have rejected the word of God. Now, instead of judging them, let's take a minute to understand why some feel the way they do. I'll be the first to say, I get it. This false image of Christ has been wickedly painted to us. This is the trick of the enemy to push us away from the true word of God and lead us down a road of destruction towards a false light.

Society tells us to find our African roots. "Do what thou wilt," let your ancestors guide you, etc. Why? Because many Blacks refuse to bow down to a "brainwashed system" that they believe was given to them by oppressors. Can I say I blame them? No, because it is a lie as it pertains to the image, but the truth lies within the word of God. Think about it, if I presented you with a gift that was wrapped in feces would you want to open it? Many will say no. What if I told you that there's pure gold in the box will you then open it? You'd probably try to dig past the crap and get to the gold. This is what the enemy does. He places something over the gift that he knows you are disgusted with, to prevent you from opening it and getting to the greatness that lies within. This is how he hides the truth. Remember you are not dealing with your average Joe, Satan is the author of lies, he is a powerful evil entity and so are his agents.

Before some start puffing up their chest with anger, let's take a deeper look at why many are disgusted with Christianity. Let's challenge ourselves to take a moment to get out of our feelings and examine things from a logical perspective. Why would someone want to bow to a God they don't identify with? Especially when there is an image of a man that resembles the ones who have oppressed Black people for ages. There are scores of white supremacists who exhibit blatant racism yet claim to be believers in Jesus Christ. They constantly antagonize and oppress God's chosen people. Many Blacks have come to view Christ as an oppressor as opposed to a savior. This perspective leads people to the conclusion that we've been conditioned and enslaved to believe a lie. Many see things from a carnal perspective versus a spiritual one. The real question is what landed us here? Why is there so much confusion? My goal is to provide you with understanding and clarity. Because as the Bible states, "My people are destroyed for lack of knowledge," Hosea 4:6, "But through knowledge, the just shall be delivered," Proverbs 11:9.

Many have never read the Bible. It is that simple. Instead, they rather listen to the perspective of others, which leads them astray. I'm not going to make this book about color. I will stand firm and address one of the tactics Satan uses to lead God's people into the world of darkness. Satan has used this false image of Christ to blind the people of God. Let's face reality, there are Blacks whose ideas, creativity, land, etc. have been stolen only to be replaced with a white man's name and face. The credit and hard work are stolen. So again, I completely understand why many struggle with reading the Bible. It is being misrepresented. I'm not going to beat anyone over the head with scripture. My goal is to challenge you to view the word of God in a different light than it is traditionally taught.

As believers, we must give understanding to others' perspectives to provide wisdom and knowledge. I understand how cunning and deceitful the enemy is. As believers, we can't be so spiritually caught up that we are no Earthly good. In other words, let's keep it real. We can't neglect to give reference to the world we live in. Do not shy away from the obvious in fear of what others may think or feel even if it brings opposition. We're addressing what many feel but never speak about openly. All of God's people will be considered outlaws when following His Law. Let's not forget a rebellious nation framed Jesus as an outlaw. Jesus himself went against common traditions and was frowned upon by society. Some happened to be the teachers of the law. According to his accusers, Jesus was defiant because he stood on God's law while defying traditions. If you are a follower of Christ you too will be hated, it comes along with the territory. "If the world hates you, keep in mind that it hated me first," John 15:18.

As a believer in Christ, I'm willing to face whatever comes my way for sharing the gospel. I see the obvious injustice being done to people of color. Many believers lack understanding so they'll randomly throw scripture at someone without taking the time to listen to how the individual feels. God is a God of patience, therefore we must show the same patience while imparting truth. The Lord knows what His people need so I lean not on my understanding but on His. I trust that He will impart the truth to His people who are lost. My job is to plant the seed and God will give the increase.

I've realized that many don't truly understand the word of God. Many label themselves as Christians but lack knowledge. Believers must get off their high horse and bring clarity to the people instead of judgment. Everyone is not crazy, they simply only see things from a carnal perspective. I don't care how much you say you believe in Christ, if you ignore history and what Blacks currently face daily in this society, then I question if you are serving the one and true living God. It is evident of the oppression Blacks have faced in this society. Before some of you get turned off and close this book after that statement, I urge you to listen to the truth. As stated previously, some people go astray and cleave to things that they can identify with. We abandon our faith which prevents God from working for us. We're then forced to rely on our power or self-will. Hence why we are still protesting and fighting to this day. Satan led us to believe the opposite of what God says, because he has many focused on a *false image*. People are being led down a road of idolatry and false god worship.

The number one goal of Satan is to attack one's faith and belief. The devil is a liar and will do anything to push you away from the truth. We should not look at a picture but instead, read the word and you will see the truth about your identity in Christ. Exodus 20:4 states, "You shall not make for yourself a carved image, or any likeness of anything that is in heaven above, or that is in the earth beneath, or that is in the water under the earth." So why are we looking at an image if the Lord himself said not to? God knew what schemes the devil would pull and He forewarned us. The sad part is many churches place false images and other wicked things in their sanctuary and expect God to dwell there. It goes completely against the word of God. Because of this, we open ourselves up to curses as this is a form of idolatry and Satanic symbols.

We as a people are fought so hard by the enemy, not just because of the color of our skin but the power that lies within. We are powerful and so is the God we serve. We lose our power when we serve other gods, participate in idol worship, follow false teachings and doctrines. The reality is that many are lost because our history has been concealed and hidden from us. The more curses placed on you the cloudier life becomes. Some will argue that the Bible is not about race. God is a spirit. You're right, God is a spirit, and we are all spiritual beings living in the natural world and being fought spiritually and physically daily. So yes, race is a factor because it is a tool Satan uses against God's people and it will not be ignored. If you are a true believer of Christ then you should know the importance of truth being revealed to set the captives free. Again, let's not dismiss the obvious in order to make people comfortable. Uncomfortable conversations are necessary at this hour.

Racism wouldn't exist if the color of one's skin was a non-factor. The truth is, race is a factor. Some will say, "A person's skin color is rarely mentioned in the Bible; the color of one's skin is meaningless to the basic message of the Bible." I truly believe we should focus on the message and the soul of man but it's hard to focus on anything spiritually when you are being fought minute by minute because of the color of your skin. If you ignore the obvious, the right prayers can never reach heaven to evoke change in the world we live in. Staying in darkness and shutting up is not a solution, especially not for believers. It's time to take action: "For the weapons of our warfare *are* not carnal but mighty in God for pulling down strongholds," 2 Corinthians 10:4.

1 Peter 2:9 states, "But you are a chosen race, a royal priesthood, a holy nation, a people for His own possession, that you may proclaim the excellencies of Him who called you out of darkness into his marvelous light." It's impossible to understand what is happening spiritually if we ignore what is happening in the physical world. Everything we face in the waking hours is a result of the warfare happening spiritually. If a race of people is enslaved physically then you can rest assured they are enslaved spiritually as well. John 8:34, "Jesus said verily verily I tell unto you everyone who sins is a slave to sin." Nothing happens on Earth without being first conceived in the realm of the spirit.

We saw this with Jacob and Esau. The Lord said to their mother who was pregnant with them at the time, "'Two nations are in your womb, and two peoples from within you will be separated; one people will be stronger than the other, and the older will serve the younger.' When the time came for her to give birth, there were twin boys in her womb. The first to come out was red, and his whole body was like a hairy garment; so they named him Esau. After this, his brother came out, with his hand grasping Esau's heel; so he was named Jacob" Genesis 23:24-26.

God has a chosen people and the descendants of those people are fought by Satan because they were chosen. "For the Lord has chosen Jacob for himself, Israel as his own possession" -Psalm 135:4. I didn't say it, scripture did. We didn't choose God, He chose us. John 15:16 states, "You did not choose me, but I chose you and appointed you that you should go and bear fruit and that your fruit should abide, so that whatever you ask the Father in my name, He may give it to you." It is important not to dismiss scripture.

We are chosen. The truth is written. King Solomon was a part of that chosen nation chosen by God. It's time to identify with scripture and not with what we were taught. If Solomon was Black how then was Jesus a white man if he was a descendant from King David? Yes, the wisest man to ever live was a BLACK MAN and there will never be another to contain his level of wisdom according to scripture. A common misconception is that there was no Black presence in scripture. Many Blacks have concluded that the Bible is a white man's book and Christianity is a white man's religion but that is a lie. Satan is the author of confusion and popularizes falsities.

Many Blacks have run away from their Christian roots to connect to the "African Culture" because the pictures that are painted of Jesus depict a white man with blue eyes and long straight hair. Many will argue that verses about Blacks were speaking "metaphorically" yet on the other hand will take every other scripture in its literal sense without debate. Let's take a moment to retrace biblical history. The book of Matthew begins Jesus' lineage with Abraham and names each father in forty-one generations ending in Matthew 1:16: "And Jacob begat Joseph the husband of Mary, of whom was born Jesus, who is called Christ." Joseph descended from David through his son Solomon. Joseph and Mary were distant cousins.

Now if King Solomon was Black and happens to be the son of King David and Jesus is a blood descendant of David then it would make him Black wouldn't it? So who created the image of a white man that is plastered and believed to be Jesus? Does color really matter? Not to me but it is relevant when it comes to truth. Satan has made Blacks believe that a white man's religion is the reason we have been enslaved. The Bible states that worshipping false gods and defying the laws of God is the reason slavery was permitted.

If the aforementioned is not enough to convince you of the Black presence in the Bible, then let me ask, who else was in slavery for 400 years? You guessed it, Blacks. "And he said unto Abram, 'Know of a surety that thy seed shall be a stranger in a land that is not theirs, and shall serve them; and they shall afflict them four hundred years,'" Genesis 15:13. The scripture said Abram was later named Abraham. Jesus is a descendant of Abraham. The worst thing you can do in life is lie to yourself about the truth inside the word of God because the lie feels better or makes others comfortable.

Many Blacks have been indoctrinated to believe that they have to look outside of the Bible to connect with their real culture when in reality Black culture is very present in the Bible. The tribes of Israel are scattered which means we are not in our native lands. Lands have been occupied by other nations which further brings confusion to our lineage. Let's not pretend that the invasion of land is some sort of conspiracy. Land has been invaded since biblical days and innocent blood was shed for it. And their "blood cries out to me from the ground." In 1 Kings 21:5-15 Naboth, the Jezreelite was killed because King Ahab wanted his vineyard for his personal desires. "Give me your vineyard, that I may have it for a vegetable garden, because it is near my house." But Naboth said to Ahab, "The Lord forbid that I should give you the inheritance of my fathers." This didn't settle well with Ahab; he was vexed, and his wife Jezebel conspired lies accusing him of cursing God and the King. Because of the false allegations, Naboth was stoned to death. After he was killed, Jezebel said to Ahab, "Arise, take possession of the vineyard of Naboth."

As you can see, this very thing has happened to our forefathers and continues to happen today. It is hard for people who have been enslaved to worship a God that resembles their slave masters. Why did I choose to bring in Jesus? I'm glad you asked. John 3:16 reminds us that God so loved the world, that He gave His only begotten son, that whosoever believeth in Him (Jesus) should not perish, but have everlasting life. Do you see the scripture come alive that states, "My people perish for a lack of knowledge?" None of this information is hidden, rather it is not widely expounded upon.

King Solomon is a descendant of King David and Christ Jesus is a descendant of King David who sits upon the throne. For thus says the LORD, "David shall never lack a man to sit on the throne of the house of Israel," Jeremiah 33:17. "Your house and your kingdom will endure forever before me; your throne will be established forever," 2 Samuel 7:16. According to the genealogy in Matthew 1, "Jesus the Messiah the son of David, the son of Abraham: Abraham was the father of Isaac, Isaac the father of Jacob." Some things are not as complex as people try to make it seem. If you follow the lineage in scripture, you will see your history. I want you to understand this background information so you can understand how we've gotten entangled in curses through misinformation.

The Bible said that "You will know them by their fruits. Grapes are not gathered from thornbushes, nor figs from thistles, are they? Even so, every good tree bears good fruit; but the bad tree bears bad fruit. A good tree cannot produce bad fruit, nor can a bad tree produce good fruit. Every tree that does not bear good fruit is cut down and thrown into the fire. So then, you will know them by their fruits," (Matthew 7:16–20). Follow scripture and examine the history, it repeats itself. How are we treated as a people? The truth is, Blacks are conditioned to believe that the Bible was the "white man's book" and Christianity is a "white" religion. Other nations saw and understood the power of the Israelites, God's chosen people. If discovering who I am offends anyone then it further proves that they are the problem. Have you noticed that making the statement "I love being Black" strikes a nerve with people just as saying "I love Jesus?" I find no coincidence there.

While tracing biblical history, let's review the story of Samson. He loses all his power when his locs are stripped. Locs are common amongst Blacks. The Bible also addresses the thickness and length of Absalom's hair, the son of King David and brother of King Solomon. Jesus' hair is also described in the Bible as hair like wool. 1 Peter 3:3 states, "Do not let your adorning be external—the braiding of hair and the putting on of gold jewelry, or the clothing you wear." Culturally Blacks are known for the braiding of hair, wearing gold jewelry, and wearing flamboyant clothing. As we explore more about hair, Absalom died while hanging in a tree. His "thick" hair got caught in the tree. Afro-textured hair is known for its thickness and density. The coarse nature of our hair harnesses strength. Many other groups have finer hair. In my mind, logic tells me that long coarse hair is strong enough to wrap around a tree and hold the body of a man. From my experience, many of my Caucasian counterparts cannot keep braids in their hair for more than a day or so without the assistance of weave because of the fine, soft nature of their tresses.

King Solomon's hair was said to be like fine gold, referring to the majesty and royalty of his hair. I find no coincidence in the story of *Goldilocks and the Three Bears*. The locs of King Solomon which were like fine gold, were turned into Goldilocks or blonde hair on a white girl to downplay and misconstrue the origins of locs. It's more than just hair. It is the altering of a narrative. The setting is in a forest. A forest is traditionally known to be the grounds where witches perform their magic. Fairytales are magical spells. Originally Goldilocks was an old white woman and later altered into a little girl. One of the most popular fairy tales in the English language. This character invades a bear family's home, eats their food, sleeps in their bed, and then disappears. The bears are described to be hospitable and trusting. These bears sound like Godly people. Nonetheless, their home was invaded by a white woman/girl much like white supremacists have done to Black people for years.

At the discovery of this, one bear says, "somebody has been lying in my bed and here she is." And in the same way, somebody has been lying about our culture, birthright, and entire lineage even tracing back biblically. According to Proverbs 6:31, "if the thief be found then he must return sevenfold." Satan has used his agents for years to manipulate the word of God and God's people. You cannot plead your case before the heavens without substantial evidence. That is why such facts are being presented before you. The people behind these "American stories" are witches and warlocks utilizing stories to cast their spells on ignorant people. Many "American stories" have British origins where many of the most powerful families are based; they are also members of the Illuminati. *Snow White* is another story of a white invasion masked as a harmless woman. Constantly stealing food and lying. Food represents the harvest of God's chosen people. Hunting rituals and ceremonies have been suggested as possible origins of these stories. Blacks have been hunted and preyed on for years and it's time to understand who we are as a people to mobilize spiritually and then physically.

No different than Christ instructing us to serve Him in the days of our youth, Satan wants that same level of fidelity. Satan wants the purity of a child to be corrupted as early as possible. As a quick reference, Delta Sigma Theta has an entire song that references the sorority ties as "a bond of our youth that keeps our hearts clean and pure til the end. The bright gleam of thy vision has lighted the world. Delta Sigma Theta our own." If that does not prove how Satan creeps in amongst gullible people seeking advancement, I don't know what will. The bright gleam of Delta is the false light of Satan. "There is no marvel, Satan transforms himself into an angel of light" but at his core is evil. If Christ is a "just" God then why is there so much injustice invoked by the same ones who claim His name? Understand that people like this want the power of God but do not want to adhere to His law. The word of God is powerful which is why many are drawn to it just as people have been drawn to Black culture because there is power in that too. I find it interesting that Blacks can easily call cultural appropriation out in the physical world but can't detect it spiritually. It's time to wake up.

We cannot turn a blind eye to what is before us. Certain people can get away with breaking the law because of the color of their skin, this will not stand in these end-days spiritually. The truth is before us, we just have to see the obvious. This type of injustice is temporal, God is allowing them to store up their iniquities before He brings them to a great fall. My prayer is that all will repent because there's a great fall coming. The system as you know it is collapsing and God's justice will prevail. True freedom will be ushered in through the Holy Spirit.

We were commanded to spread the gospel to ALL nations so that all may be saved, but Satan brings division by corrupting nations and distracting us with a false image, leading many away from the real word of God. I believe if Satan had the power he would have gotten rid of the Bible in its entirety. But he does not have that type of authority when it comes to the word of God. God said His word stands and will not be touched so it will forever remain. The author of lies has limits on what he can do. He depicts false images and narratives so the word can be rejected by the chosen people of God. He understood people would not bow and worship a god that looks like a descendant of those who have oppressed them and their ancestors. This is how Satan deceives people.

If you had a child and he or she was kidnapped and the kidnapper changed their hair color, clothes and altered the child's overall image. Would you want your child back if you knew where to find him/her or will you say throw the child away? A good parent will get their child regardless. So don't throw away the word of God because Satan tries to uproot what's yours. The word of God is where your power lies. Satan knew that, hence why he brought confusion. Let me give you another example: in modern-day society, if a white man was healing others would that upset people enough to want to hang him from a cross? Would society wrongfully accuse him of being a criminal when he was not? I think not. However, if a Black man was healing people I'm sure they would find something wrong with it. They'd probably say things like "where is his medical license, he's not even licensed. Lock him up and throw away the key." People are so religious that they do not face reality. God gave us wisdom for a reason. Before anything takes place in the natural, it first is conceived in the spiritual. Which race of people have been known to unjustly be hung from trees? Blacks. Just as Jesus was hung on the cross. The lies told to Blacks for generations are the reason this point is being driven.

Have you ever stopped to think, maybe they crucify Christ in the flesh every time they crucify his descendants? I have, and it makes perfect sense. Galatians 3:13 says "Christ redeemed us from the curse of the law by becoming a curse for us. For it is written: Cursed is everyone who is hung on a tree." He redeemed us so that the blessing promised to Abraham would come to the Gentiles in Christ Jesus so that by faith we might receive the promise of the Spirit. It must be understood that there were curses placed on us as Blacks because of our rebellion and our ancestors who formed evil altars. These agents of Satan desire God's people to live in a curse so that the blessings of God will never manifest in their lives.

Yes, Christ has redeemed us from the curse of the law by becoming a curse for us. However, this is not a free pass to continue in evil. We cannot turn to idolatry and expect Christ's mercy to continue to abide in our lives. "What shall we say then? Shall we continue in sin, that grace may abound?" Romans 6:1. The goal for Satan is to get us back into bondage and the only way to do that is by defying God's law. That in itself leads to self-destruction. Our non-belief will land us in the hands of Satan every time. It's time to fight for our birthright. It's scripture, God made a covenant with Abraham so when we align with God, we will be partakers of the blessings. Rest assured that the enemy works overtime to keep us from those promises.

Bringing this back to present-day society, oppressors never wanted Blacks to be superheroes even though our roots trace back to being kings and queens. They didn't want their children looking up to us or aspiring to be like us. They'd rather dumb us down forcing us to believe our best Superhero reflects the traits of the character known as "Blankman." Some may not be familiar with the 1994 American superhero comedy parody film. Blankman is not a marvel film hero with elite powers but rather a Black man who's a fan of Batman. In the film, he's depicted as a repairman who's clumsy, childlike, and mindless. Just as they want the Black man to be portrayed. A man without a mind solely depending on Satan and his wicked disciples to tell us who we are by erasing our history. That ultimately makes us a "Blankman." Oftentimes the truth is hidden in comedy to distract us from reality. History shows us that we only serve as amusement and mockery to other nations for their entertainment. In the movie, Blankman was self-labeled a Black superhero but had no real power at all, coincidence much? Make mockery of our real strength through ignorance and jokes. You should ask yourself who runs the entertainment industry as a whole. It's definitely not Blacks. Some Blacks have been compensated to push an agenda and serve as agents in Satan's sanctuary. That's the unfortunate truth we live in.

The same people who hate us want to capture the power of God that is fueling us. There would be no better way to do that than to strip us from our power source. Confuse God's people with an image that looks nothing like Him. God's people have been brainwashed to believe their oppressors created a belief system called Christianity to keep Blacks bound. In all actuality, the word of God was designed for people to be free through Christ Jesus. It is no secret that enslaved people were beaten and killed for reading. I doubt that they were trying to read frivolous novels and magazines. The word of God is freedom and these agents of Satan knew that. Jealousy toward the Black race still exists today and the tactics are not new, the times have simply changed.

The world of the occult is big on colors. Colors communicate messages subtly and channel energy. Even as God instructed King Solomon to build the tabernacle. The Lord was precise with the numbers for measurements of items and specific colors for the articles the house of God should contain. These secret societies that govern the world follow suit. The color of Black people's skin communicated a message of royalty and kingship in biblical days. Now that has been altered by oppressors, making Blacks seemingly indicative of a lower class. They have brainwashed our society into believing all sorts of lies and this particular lie is a terrible falsehood that has augmented reality for Black's worldwide.

Just as God is mysterious, and so is His chosen nation, our peculiar nature has scientists working overtime to understand what's in our DNA. I believe that God placed supernatural powers inside of His people and it will manifest itself in the last days. "And it shall come to pass in the last days, saith God, I will pour out My Spirit upon all flesh; and your sons and your daughters shall prophesy, and your young men shall see visions, and your old men shall dream dreams," Acts 2:17. Understand that "all" refers to all who believe in Him and are called by His name. Before Christ, Israel was His chosen holy nation. Later, salvation would be extended not only to the Jews but the Gentiles as well. When people say we are all chosen, that's not what scripture says. Other nations have all been extended grace, but in the beginning, there was a chosen people handpicked by God called the Israelites and their descendants are scattered far and wide today. The only thing that can stop God's power from flowing in us is our disobedience to Him. We are our own demise. From the beginning of time Blacks have been the most powerful race both physically, mentally, and spiritually. We lose our power when we rebel against God.

There's an evident reason why we are the most hated yet most appropriated culture in the world. Those who deny this often say "does everything have to be about race with you people?" They don't want to face the reality we and our ancestors had to face. The only way to get our strength back is not through protesting but repenting and renouncing our idols. "If my people, which are called by my name, shall humble themselves, and pray, and seek my face, and turn from their wicked ways; then will I hear from heaven, and will forgive their sin, and will heal their land," 2 Chronicles 7:14. Let us not rebel and hate one another because it never ends well.

Be proud of who you are. God's people are the most powerful beings walking this Earth, we are the scattered tribes of Israel. Now let me be clear because I know how people like to twist words and paint a negative picture of the truth. Me loving my culture doesn't mean I hate others. Christ does not intend for us to hate but rather pray for those who curse us. I spread this truth from a pure place and as mentioned before I will not withhold truth to make anyone comfortable. I am shedding light on subjects that have God's people bound. It is time for the lost to be found and we must know who we are so we can better understand who God is. We were made in His image and not in the image of man-made things. It is hard for people to identify with an image that does not look like them so they reject the truth. This cycle of lies ends now.

There is ethnicity all through scripture including names. Speaking of names, let's address the other senseless debates. I have a first name, middle name, last name, and several nicknames. If someone calls me by any of my names, I'm going to answer. Although I have several names I'm the same person, as it is with Christ. This should not be a debate because it takes us further from Him. If you prefer Emmanuel, Yeshua, Yahweh, Jehovah, Hosanna, Elohim, El Shaddai, whatever your native tongue is, speak His name. In (English) Jesus, (Hebrew)Yehoshua, (Chinese) Yēsū Jīdū, (Haitian Creole) Jezikri, (Spanish) Jesucristo, (Russian) Iisus Khristos. It's all the same, we should not be distracted with senseless debates but instead focusing on the word of God, which He honors above His name. "For thou hast magnified thy word above all thy name," Psalm 138:2. Whatever you call the master, just make sure you worship Him in spirit and truth. My God uses many names and they ALL hold power.

All law-abiding believers will taste the grace no matter what color you are or what language you speak. There will be many nations that stand before the Lord. Revelation 7:9 says, "After this I looked, and behold, a great multitude that no one could number, from every nation, from all tribes and peoples and languages, standing before the throne and before the Lamb, clothed in white robes, with palm branches in their hands." The goal is to spend eternity with God and until we get that opportunity, we must live in truth by rightfully dividing the word of God holding no man captive. By captive, I also mean not withholding their history. God is not pleased with that.

Journal Entry

Lord today I came to the altar seeking answers. I've reached my peak. I don't understand what you want from me. Are you even listening? I am unsure if I'm hearing from you or is it my desire that is causing me to think, dream and envision what my future should be. I feel so lost. I need confirmation, Jesus. I've prayed to you for clarity. I need answers Lord, and I need them NOW. My mind is exhausted. I'm tossing and turning while trying to sleep. It feels like I'm never rested and what should be understood is confusing. What I feel in the natural doesn't align with what you are telling me. God, I'm trying to trust you but my flesh is becoming more aggravated by the day. So I question, did I waste years praying about what you promised me? I don't feel a connection to my purpose. My fight comes from pride. The idea of being wrong is causing me to feel confused and hurt. I don't know if my pride and self-will are overpowering Your will. Did you really say that or is my mind being controlled? How can you promise good things when I'm experiencing bad things? I'm so confused and I came to the altar today seeking direction. I'm tired of doubting and emotionally I'm all over the place. I looked at myself in the mirror searching for the God inside of me. I came with the expectation to get an answer with the help of my prayer partner. She anointed me as she walked around the church covering each corner ushering the Holy Spirit in as I prayed. My body felt weak as I prayed. I couldn't seem to reach You. My head began to hurt like never before and my body felt sick. I couldn't call out. War was being waged spiritually. It was time for spiritual birthing and something needed to be broken but I couldn't tap in. So I laid down and fell asleep for several hours and awoke around 2am, my head was still hurting. I felt helpless and tired in the natural and in the spiritual. I stood in the mirror to see what You see. I knew there was something I needed to birth spiritually. I couldn't walk around with a seed in me without pushing through. I didn't want it to die inside of me. I went back to the altar and laid for a few more hours (4am —6am) before giving a final push to tap in spiritually. As I prayed, my spirit began to break and I realized this birth was about me and God. This was not about trying to figure things out but rather being obedient to what God had spoken. As I focused on Jesus, I still felt weak physically. After hours of praying, I heard the Holy Spirit say, "I knew you before you were in the womb." He said He "has plans to prosper me and give me hope in the future, not to harm me." It was so clear, The Lord sent angels in the delivery room when my mother was giving birth to me. There was a fight in the spirit that took place when I was born. I then saw in a vision the spirit of me walking down a long empty hall calling out, "Elohim, what is it that you want? What is your will? Who am I?" I could see a bright light. I heard the Holy Spirit say, "you were born for a purpose. I've invested in you." I was bowing down crying. The Holy Spirit then said, "you are now in your prime to be a Queen. I made you to rule." His promise came back to me, "Your talents I shall bless, I shall give you great wisdom and understanding." I felt I was being crowned in the spirit. The Holy Spirit said, "walk towards me." I remember feeling tired and I wanted Him to carry me, but He said, "walk." I felt like a child taking their first steps. The Holy Spirit said to walk in the light. I walked towards the light and I felt His presence. I fell into His arms just after a few steps. The spiritual birth happened, and I cried out to God. What seemed so hard to do, strangely became so easy. I could feel the comfort of the Holy Spirit as I cried, not wanting to let Him go. I didn't care about the details, this push was for "me." That day I got more than I expected. "A meeting with Jesus" is an experience I will forever remember. My one-on-one with Him confirmed my purpose here on Earth (the most important thing I could ever know). I am a Queen on assignment for the Lord, so GLORY to your name, I thank you, Jesus.

    I must now have the mindset of a Queen. The Holy Spirit told me to revisit the timeline entry on July 17, 2014, and there I will find my answer. Jesus, my friend, my King, my Father, my savior, my redeemer, my peace, my protector, my light, my lamb, my lion, my leader, my teacher, my everything. I love you JESUS, thank you God for your son.

                      Love The King's Daughter
                        The Daughter of a KING
                                  -Crys
                                7/17/2015

Journal Entry

Today I realize I must follow my calling and not my dreams. I understand that there's a difference at this point. Each day I battle with following God's will while resisting my flesh. This walk is far from easy but I'm striving. I'm young, I can have anything I want if I chose to take that route. But I'm really trying to see it through, you know, stay in the paint with God. I sometimes feel like much of what I'm doing is in vain. God are you punishing me or am I being pruned? I'm nowhere near where I thought I would be by now but I guess that's the way life goes. I'm about to be another age in a few weeks and I'm praying that new things begin to happen. Feel like me again, feel accomplished, actually not struggle with paying bills. This is becoming a lot. I wish I could say that I know for sure that everything is going to be alright but I don't feel it. Yeah, that's where I'm at.

> Not sure but I'm here and I know that God is somewhere up there.
>
> Love The King's Daughter
> The Daughter of a KING
> -Crys
> 9/5/2015

7

"The curses they brought upon themselves fell on me."
GENERATIONAL CURSES

In so many cases we cannot experience the fullness of God because of the entanglements in our lives. Some of you may say, well I have never served another god but perhaps you have. Putting ANYTHING above Jesus Christ is called idolatry. Many have fallen victim to putting a significant other, child(ren), a job, tarot card readings, you name it, above Christ and entered into a curse. Yet again, anything we exalt above the law of God levies a curse. For many who say, "that has not been my case," well great. However, let's take a moment to check your history.

IDENTIFYING THE CURSES:

Think back in your life to various things you have been or are involved with. Do you identify with zodiacs? Have you gone for a palm or tarot card reading? Do you sage your home to get rid of evil spirits? Did you have sexual intercourse with someone who wasn't your husband or wife? Are you currently fornicating? Are you living a life of homosexuality? Have you allowed another man or woman into your marriage via a threesome? Have you or your family members joined occult organizations? These are hardcore questions that need answers if healing and deliverance will take place. Write these things down in a journal, recount dates, and incidences so that you can confess your sins before the Lord and be direct about the deliverance you are seeking. This is a time to reflect. Especially if you have children or plan to have them because their quality of life will be affected by every choice you make and have made.

Much of what was discussed are "known sins," however many still lack understanding about horoscopes and zodiacs. As believers, the only signs we should be following are the miracles, signs, and wonders of Jesus Christ. Following zodiacs has become a thing that "everybody does" but I want to reassure you, just because many do it does not make it right. The Bible reminds us that broad is the road that leads to destruction.

Satan mimics everything God does as we've established earlier in this book. God created twelve tribes. Satan created twelve signs. It's Babylonian astrology and you're welcome to do your research. What does the Bible tell us about Babylon? In the book of revelation "Babylon the great, is the mother of prostitutes and of Earth's abominations." I get it! We've been forced to believe in the man-made signs placed upon us at birth. Trust me, I used to be the first to represent being a "Libra" until God used a friend to reveal to me the evil basis of these signs.

Each sign is a demonic entity all based upon astrology. In certain seasons certain demons are released. There is a time and season for everything under the sun. People born during a certain season would indeed have likened characteristics, but each person is an individual and chooses their paths and will have to work out his/her soul's salvation. Each time you "rep your sign" you're pledging allegiance to that demon. The more you do it the more the spirit is invited into your life, this is no different than worshiping God. The more you worship Him the more He pours His spirit into you. I want to provide enlightenment to those who are unaware as I was. When the Lord says my people perish for a lack of knowledge, this too is a part of our ignorance that is causing us to die without living in the freedom of God. Getting your freedom involves renouncing everything that keeps you bound. When people ask what sign I am, I now say

"Child of God." I don't fear people thinking "I'm too deep" because I'm free. A slave wouldn't understand the thoughts of a free man.

If by any chance you think what I'm saying is too far off I want to provide you with a biblical reference of what God feels about horoscopes/astrology. "All the counsel you have received has only worn you out! Let your astrologers come forward, those stargazers who make predictions month by month, let them save you from what is coming upon you." Isaiah 47:13. Do you find it ironic that these zodiacs are assigned based on one's birth date? That in itself should highlight how Satan is after the children of God's birthright.

While on the subject of birthright blessings, many of us were born into curses unknowingly. You see, even after repenting and renouncing the organization, the Holy Spirit spoke to me in a dream stating, "there is still witchcraft in your life." I was utterly perplexed because anything that I was in I made a conscious effort to get out. When I got that dream, I immediately went on a 3-day dry fast because I needed answers and more so, I needed to be unbound from those evil altars. I discovered that this form of witchcraft was the result of ancestral curses that were still controlling my destiny. The Holy Spirit pointed me back to a particular instance in my childhood and showed me as clear as day, the very altar where certain curses were initially evoked which was in my household.

I was a child when I was taken to a woman's house who was known to delve into witchcraft. When I got home, I noticed a red bowl filled with water. In this bowl, there was a piece of paper with several names written in red ink. The bowl was placed in the back of the freezer and left for months. One day the bowl was removed from the freezer and I was told not to touch it as it defrosted on the countertop. I was inquisitive and quite advanced so I read all the names I could make out. I can still remember a few that were written down. Even then as a small child something in my spirit knew it wasn't right which is probably why I can still remember this account 'til this day. I'm fully aware in my spiritual maturity today that there was witchcraft being done in the form of a freezer spell. This type of spell shuts your enemies down if they are gossiping, spreading rumors, or trying to ruin your life. It is designed to stop them in their tracks or freeze their actions. Something that was done for "protection" levied a curse that I would come to live in although I had nothing to do with it. Attempting to freeze someone would later freeze the members of the household as the cycle of life continued. This is proven in Numbers 14:18, "The LORD is longsuffering and abundant in mercy, forgiving iniquity and transgression; but He by no means clears the guilty, visiting the iniquity of the fathers on the children to the third and fourth generation."

The world of witchcraft is very powerful and those who do not understand it will become a victim of it. As I reflect, witchcraft did not just start once I crossed over into the world of the occult, but it showed itself forth even in my early childhood. Let me give you an example of just how witchcraft can be levied against you at any stage of your life. I was in elementary school and succeeded in anything I did academically. There was one particular boy who always had a competitive nature against me. From spelling bees to building puzzles, you name it and he made it a competition. That bred jealousy and hate toward me. One day we were in our music class being assigned instruments. Since I was the tallest student in our class and possessed the ability to handle the larger instrument, my music teacher assigned me the instrument that this boy was secretly hoping for. As he retrieved his instrument he was fuming with anger. All of the students were standing up assembling their instruments. All of a sudden he came by my desk and kicked me in the knee. Now, this was no ordinary kick because he was skilled in karate. At that moment I knew I had to defend myself. We got into a physical fight in our music class. He was badly bruised as the school security pulled me off of him and we were both pending a suspension.

My mother took me to the hospital to find I had sustained a fractured knee from his initial kick. There were several conferences between both of our mothers and the school officials to discuss the consequences. After the full investigation, he was proven to be the aggressor and was suspended. The boy's mother was furious and wanted revenge. As usual, my mother picked me up from school. She typically came into the class and that day she continued her routine in doing so. As we walked outside my mother noticed a knitted female voodoo doll wearing an orange dress with a broken arm. My mother asked the school security if she saw anyone near her car and the security officer affirmed that the boy's mother had placed the doll on the hood of her car. She flung the doll off of her car, reported it to the school officials, and proceeded with our day.

A couple of weeks later I was playing with a classmate on her porch a few blocks away from my school when I fell and broke my arm. Ironically, I was wearing an orange dress just as it appeared on that voodoo doll. This proves that the curses that are levied can prevail if there is a reason for them to take precedence in your life. Proverbs 26:2 reminds us that "Like a fluttering sparrow or a darting swallow, an undeserved curse will not land on its intended victim." If there is any loophole then those curses will have legal jurisdiction under spiritual law to run their course. Clearly, in my situation, there was a door open spiritually which gave grounds for the witchcraft to take root. Generational curses were the access point in my life. You must rid yourself of all evil covenants through the knowledge of God, and through fasting and prayer so the weapons of Satan do not prosper against you.

Do not be deceived. There are family members who have participated in witchcraft and Satanic practices where they erected altars and those very same altars may be permeating curses and speaking to your destiny even as you read this book. These curses, as stated earlier, transcend to the third and fourth generation according to biblical teachings. The question at hand is, what did mom, dad, aunty, uncle, cousin, grandpa, and grandma do for prosperity or protection? Which family member sacrificed you for their gain? Who was/ is consulting with the dead for guidance and instruction? These questions are not being pondered to see who you are going to chew out for doing so but rather to untie your destiny and walk fully into who God called you to be before the foundations of the Earth.

These covenants that were made by family members are called ancestral curses and show themselves differently from family to family and from person to person. Some curses come in the form of non-marriage or failed marriages/divorces and for many, there is a long family history to prove it. Other curses cause entire bloodlines to lead a life of misery, never experiencing the positive side of life.

The more God enlightened me, I felt rather deceived and misguided as I was taught to believe that once you are "washed by the blood of Jesus" that was the only faith you needed. That is not it. Yes, Jesus paid the ultimate sacrifice so that we may have life and live more abundantly, but at the same time there is a huge fight at hand when curses are plaguing your bloodline and evil covenants are being entered every day. That entangles us all the more. Where it is a fact that some curses you are living in are not a result of what you have done, unfortunately, you have every responsibility to untie yourself if you desire to be free and experience a better quality of life. If you are dealing with any form of lack in your life you must identify the root cause and attack it spiritually.

8

"Realigning with God's will."
GETTING OUT

I had to repent, renounce spiritually and physically the covenant I made, and fast and pray to be fully released. The process of getting out was just as much of a headache as it was to get in. Between having to write a letter, calling every day to the headquarters to get a response from the membership chair, being on a waiting list, to having an official counseling call, being told once I renounced I could never seek membership again in Delta Sigma Theta, getting official documents notarized, waiting six to eight weeks to get the paperwork stating that I was officially off of the roster of members, this was a long journey, to say the least. I fought to get through the pledge process and nothing would hold me back from gaining my freedom no matter what confronted me. What I went through physically does not even scratch the surface regarding what I was spiritually dealing with. Whenever you break a covenant Satan wants you back at all costs. There is a constant battle to hold fast to your faith when it seems like all hell breaks loose as you break through.

    Some who are inactive members believe they are free. But according to spiritual law and even the doctrines of these Greek letter organizations, they are still under a contract which means they are bound. You have to break that contract both spiritually and physically. In the same respect, a divorce is not final until the paperwork is signed and processed in due form. For those wondering, it is just that serious. An inactive member is still a member who is in bondage. It's likened to being a prisoner who has chosen to be silent. Telling someone you're not a part of the organization anymore because you're inactive is like saying, "I don't participate with the other inmates, I stay in my cell while they are out on the yard." Again, that's not being FREE, they're still in bondage.

I love reading about the account of Apostle Paul in Ephesus in the book of Acts 18:20: "Many of those who believed now came and openly confessed what they had done. A number who had practiced sorcery brought their scrolls together and burned them publicly. When they calculated the value of the scrolls, the total came to fifty thousand drachmas. In this way, the word of the Lord spread widely and grew in power." Just as the witches and warlocks burnt their scrolls, I took every piece of paraphernalia, my ritual book, and all of the other articles about Delta and set them on fire. That was such a big moment for me. I had more elephants than I cared to count, scores of shirts, jackets, sorority pins, flowers, and other memorabilia. Being in the organization for nearly a decade I had a huge shrine of items and all of it had to go expeditiously. I had them on display in my home not knowing that every piece contained spirits sacrificed unto a false god. The process of getting rid of everything was surreal. I could not believe I had sacrificed so much just to end up cursed by defying God as that was never my initial goal. I shed a few tears and rejoiced that I had broken the curses through the power of God, never to be bound by anything like that again.

The more I began to break these curses and covenants, the more I became attacked in my dreams by demonic forces. I've experienced countless occasions of what is known as sleep paralysis, where an evil force was pinning me down, preventing me from waking up. I literally would be fighting in my dream and the only thing that broke me free from the demonic attacks was my ability to say the name, Jesus. Even trying to utter the name Jesus was a struggle. That is how I know that there is power in the name of Jesus because when I would say His name instantly I would break free from that stronghold keeping me bound in that dream. I would have to wake up, pray and renounce any covenants that were seeking to reestablish me in Satan's kingdom. In Matthew 13:25 it states, "But while men slept, his enemy came and sowed tares among the wheat, and went his way." This showcases how Satan uses subtle devices even through dreams to get our consent to establish or reestablish evil covenants. There is constantly a battle going on in the unseen world and while the physical body rests, the spirit is still awake, warring. The spirit cannot fight if not suited with the full armor of God. Understanding the use of each piece of spiritual equipment is pivotal. Before resting, be it for a nap or a full night's sleep, as believers we must gird ourselves with the full armor by speaking it over ourselves and our families.

Ephesians 6:11-19 states, "Put on the whole armour of God, that ye may be able to stand against the wiles of the devil. For we wrestle not against flesh and blood, but against principalities, against powers, against the rulers of the darkness of this world, against spiritual wickedness in high places. Wherefore take unto you the whole armour of God, that ye may be able to withstand in the evil day, and having done all, to stand. Stand therefore, having your loins girt about with truth, and having on the breastplate of righteousness; And your feet shod with the preparation of the gospel of peace. Above all, taking the shield of faith, wherewith ye shall be able to quench all the fiery darts of the wicked. And take the helmet of salvation, and the sword of the Spirit, which is the word of God: Praying always with all prayer and supplication in the Spirit, and watching thereunto with all perseverance and supplication for all saints; And for me, that utterance may be given unto me, that I may open my mouth boldly, to make known the mystery of the gospel."

Journal Entry

Choosing Victory

Today I had myself a good cry, took off my bra, tied up my hair, and had myself a good cry. As an extraordinary woman, I sometimes forget that I too am a common girl with ordinary problems. The weight of the world seems to be playing tug of rope with my heart today. Sometimes I question God and ask Him why He made me this way? Why am I concerned with everyone being pleased even if it comes at the expense of my feelings? Why do I treat myself like a machine and not a human being? Why am I gentle with everyone else except for myself? Why do I try to encourage others even when I feel broken? Today, I'm just plain out tired and overwhelmed... with life, people, things, feelings of past hurt, yesterday, last week, and even by tomorrow. I just need to release! And I am choosing today because if I keep going through life dealing with situations and never truly healing, I will self-destruct. After hours upon hours of crying, puffy eyes, a red nose, and a soaked t-shirt, I realized that the problem was not with people and the truth is, it will never be. My issues are within me. I am fighting against who my flesh wants me to be and who God has called me to be. Truth be told, it doesn't feel good when we're mistreated, especially when you pour out your heart to people. Shoot, that makes the old Crys want to resurrect from the dead, and that's real. At Bible study, Bishop taught us about becoming submissive to death just as Christ did. My flesh says, "Well, I ain't Jesus," but my spirit understands "no cross, no crown." This essentially means that if I forfeit the suffering, I forfeit inheriting the kingdom and all of the riches Christ has for me. What's a queen without her crown of glory? Today, I realize that I am keeping things on life support in my life that God is trying to pull the plug on. The lesson is that I must die daily so that God can fulfill His perfect work in my life. So I pose this rhetorical question, if I know the word of God, practice it, and have received prophecies about the ordination of my life, then why am I still struggling spiritually? Immediately I heard First Lady's words, "Baby, it all starts with the mind. Changing your mental state will change the course of your life." Wise words from a wise woman! I receive that word and activate it in my spirit. These are words I have chosen to live by. I guess God is dealing with me on expectations and attitudes. For years I have had unrealistic expectations of others and myself. In situations where my expectations were not met, it, in turn, weighed on my heart causing a shift in my attitude. Guilt, doubt, disappointment, and feelings of being less than are commonly felt thereafter. However, I am learning daily that there is no need to beat myself up when I don't meet my expectations or the expectations of others. God expects progress, not perfection. I realize that I can be my own worst critic, leaving my best to never be good enough. But as long as I operate in the spirit of love and do everything unto God that is all that matters. Today I seek divine revelation on sticking to my position in Christ no matter what my current condition is. I choose victory even when the enemy presents defeat. I put my feet to my faith by taking up my sword and fighting with the word of God. Thus, I declare these faith professions over my life:

- I am the head and not the tail, I am above and not beneath.

- I can do all things through Christ which strengthens me.
- I will not get weary in well doing, for in due season I will reap my harvest if I faint not.
- I will consider Christ who endured such heavy afflictions and sufferings before I feel entitled to mope in my pity.
- I will give, expecting nothing in return from man but my reward from God as the word declares, "Give and it shall be given unto you good measure, pressed down shaken together running over."
- I will wake up, pray, and slay!
- I will laugh out loud and smile even when I feel bruised. Why? Because this confuses the enemy.
- I will write the vision and make it plain because the Lord honors His word above His name.
- I will boldly stand amid judgment because I have a great high priest petitioning on my behalf and His track record proves that He is undefeated.
- I will fight for every promise and blessing that is due to me in this lifetime.
- I will give respect to seasons knowing that there will be sunshine as well as rain.

- I will operate in the spirit of gratefulness and will sow good seeds expecting my harvest from Christ
- I will never dim the light that God has placed over my life to accommodate others. For in doing this I displease my father and mishandle that in which He has charged me to steward over.
- I will continue to encourage others in their gifts as Philippians 2:3 teaches: "Don't be selfish; don't try to impress others. Be humble, thinking of others as better than yourselves."

Daughter of a KING
The KING'S Daughter
-Crys
9/23/2015

9

"Don't touch my hair."
THE CURSES LEVIED ON THE CROWN

Culturally, hair is a major deal for us. Scripture teaches us that a woman's hair is her crown of glory. Undoubtedly there has always been a fascination with the texture of Black hair throughout history so much that we're constantly asked, "Can I touch your hair?" Anything that brings us glory will be attacked spiritually and manifest itself physically which is for both men and women alike. I believe before the onset of curses placed on the people of God, our hair flourished because it held great power. Satan understands that and seeks to attack the head. I dream often, and one very vivid dream I woke up yelling. There was a black vicious cat with green eyes digging its paws into the center of my head. This cat had its sharp teeth and tongue exposed as it sought to kill me. My hands were fully extended over my head while gripping its body. I was fighting to get this cat's paws out of the center of my head. Although I could see a cat it felt like I was fighting a human. I woke up grunting, screaming, and breathing heavily. I was under spiritual attack and did not know it. This was around the time I would experience the worst attack on my scalp and skin and would also begin losing more of my tangible possessions.

As I have said, dreams are an eye gate into the spiritual realm. Because of the evil altars I was already bound to, these demonic spirits had jurisdiction to launch an attack on me. During that time frame, my scalp was in so much pain. Believe it or not, blood and pus secreted from my scalp.

I experienced unnatural hair loss. God had blessed me with a clean and clear face but I began to have cystic acne that would hurt even when it wasn't touched. Many of us through ignorance have dreams that we do not fully interpret. It is through our dreams that many evil covenants are formed spiritually which manifests itself in our waking. The spirits attacking me wanted to strangle the life out of me and had it not been for God they would have. The attack was specifically placed in the crown of my head and that is where I experienced the worst pain, breakage, and pimples. Many women and even men have experienced extreme hair loss or been diagnosed with a scalp condition. People spend hundreds of dollars seeking medical advice but never come to a resolution. The attack that is experienced must be handled at its core first and that is spiritual.

Many of us have sat in salons and unknowingly become victims of witchcraft attacks. A friend of mine was experiencing migraine headaches, extreme loss of hair, and chronic scalp pain. Her scalp would be in so much pain that she would physically become sick, oftentimes vomiting from the way she felt. She could not wear hairstyles for more than three days or so and her life had truly changed with this new condition. She went to dermatologists, spent hundreds of dollars on prescribed remedies, underwent red laser therapy but the situation persisted. She described that the pain in her scalp felt as if something was constantly biting it. It was not until she went on a three-day dry fast, did the Holy Spirit reveal to her via a dream that a family friend who had previously been her stylist took pieces of her hair and used it to place witchcraft on her. Because of the generational curses that were in effect this witchcraft worked. The Lord showed her the hair that was taken from her displayed on a large board. She became free of that curse and so many others through prayer, fasting, and the spirit of God. Her hair and scalp are now flourishing at their natural state and are healthier than they have ever been. The altar that was set up, permeated curses on this woman's scalp and altered her life.

THE SPIRIT OF SHIANDA

The purpose of sharing this is to show you how we oftentimes fight everything physically first, forgetting, or in some people's cases not understanding, that things manifested physically have already been conceived spiritually. If you want to know the source of your problems, you must plug into the source which is Christ Jesus. We must be aware of who we allow to touch our crowns. Stylists and barbers are not exempt from being witches and warlocks. The spirit of jealousy and greed causes people to do ungodly things to those who patronize their businesses. It does not matter how sweet and genuine a person appears, you must ask God for direction in all aspects of your life as you could be another sacrifice on someone's altar.

PERSONAL REFLECTION:

What dreams have you had that didn't quite add up in your mind? Have you ever had a dream and you felt there was a clear message for you but couldn't figure it out?

_____

_____

_____

_____

_____

PERSONAL REFLECTION:

Now that you have reflected on those moments. Go back to that actual time frame in your mind. What feelings came over you? Were you scared, anxious, or did you feel a sense of warmth and comfort? As you reflect, what was happening in your waking life during that time frame?

_____

_____

_____

_____

PERSONAL REFLECTION:

Is there anything outlined in this book that brought revelation to what God was trying to reveal to you? List the symbols and comparisons.

_____

_____

_____

_____

10

"Dreams are the eye-gate into the spiritual world."

NOTHING HAPPENS PHYSICALLY BEFORE BEING SPIRITUALLY CONCEIVED

> Acts 2:17-22 — "In the last days, God says, I will pour out My Spirit on all people.
> Your sons and daughters will prophesy,
> your young men will see visions,
> your old men will dream dreams.
> Even on My menservants and maidservants
> I will pour out My Spirit in those days,
> and they will prophesy.
> I will show wonders in the heavens above
> and signs on the earth below,
> blood and fire and billows of smoke.
> The sun will be turned to darkness,
> and the moon to blood,
> before the coming of the great and glorious Day of the Lord.
> And everyone who calls on the name of the Lord
> will be saved."

If you have noticed, I refer to dreams quite often throughout this book because God uses dreams and visions to enlighten His people on what is to come. The same God that spoke to His people in the Bible is doing the same for us today. I am a firm believer that God frees people so they can help free others. Another revelation given by the Lord came in a dream during the height of the COVID-19 pandemic. Before I laid down for bed, the Holy Spirit said, "you will see lines in the sky appearing as black ink." While dreaming, I then saw the sky turn pitch black. There was a light around what appeared as black ink in the sky. Words began to fly around that read WAH, WOW, WAKE THEM. In this dream, I was in my car where I usually shoot my motivational videos. These powerful words bounced off the windshield. I was with my prayer partner in this dream. Although it was pitch black, God gave me a supernatural vision to see the words through the darkness. I said with excitement, "look, it's here!" In the waking hours, we ended that same night with prayer before the dream. Her words to God were, "Lord we are tired, but we do not need to be asleep while you are trying to minister to us." This dream was powerful because God revealed what I would see before I saw it.

Let's shift to the revelation behind the dream. WAH is an acronym for working at home. WOW is an acronym for the world of witchcraft. The Holy Spirit gave me a command to wake the people plagued by the effects of witchcraft working against them from within their homes and universally. That detail where the Holy Spirit said the lines would appear as black ink let me know that what we perceive with the human eye is not always what something truly is at its core. Black ink in this dream indicated deception. Just as the scripture in 2 Corinthians 11:14, "And no marvel; for Satan himself is transformed into an angel of light."

God was showing that the people were under a great deception. Scripture teaches that even the elect will be deceived. The spirit of fear causes many to abandon faith. We bore witness to this during the pandemic. There were people of God panicking more than they were praying. I received divine orders. God freed me from the world of the occult and generational curses, and I was given the duty of freeing His people. It was time to mobilize and send a loud cry into the land to spread God's truth and help people break the curses over their lives.

My dreams are coming more frequently and more vividly which lets me know that time is running out. The coming of the Lord is near. God has been revealing the interpretations of these dreams and they have been mind-blowing. One particular night, I had a dream of being at the same location my Delta line had our coming out show. I was walking and saw two of my former line sisters. They were sobbing, crying, and in distress while sitting in the amphitheater. I stopped and looked at them with concern, then asked what was wrong. Neither one of them could speak, they seemed to cry harder. I looked up and saw the most devastating sight. There was a light pole that extended upward about 120 plus feet up to the sky. Balanced on this light pole was a large plank of wood. On the wooden plank were dozens of Deltas tightly standing and all dressed in red suits.

They were being forced to jump off the plank two by two with no harness. There was a great fall that resulted in death. I understood immediately why the two were crying. They understood their destiny. In another scene of the dream, I saw others who are not Greek affiliated but are in the world of witchcraft jumping from a ledge two by two. I awoke from the dream very troubled in my spirit. I poured out to God on their behalf praying that their souls would be saved.

The Lord showed me these women on a light pole because the god of this world, Satan, has led them down the road of false light. The false light led them to a high place only to be destroyed, as sheep led blindly to the slaughterhouse. The goal of Satan is to kill, steal, and destroy. Unfortunately, we co-conspire with Satan in many regards to kill our destiny and defy the laws of God. The dream where the women of Delta were on that light pole reminded me of the Odyssey Experience back when I was a pyramid. We walked across tightropes about thirty feet in the air. What I saw in the dream was not just an experience. It was the ultimate fate of these women. Everyone who partakes in the world of darkness must make a decision.

Time is of the essence. According to Exodus 22:18-19, all witches will be put to death. Death and hell is the punishment for witchcraft.

This information can be much to digest for the average person but use this resource as a guide to attack what has been controlling your life from a spiritual stance not carnally. This book is not a one-time read but rather composed to be a foundation to help you build your strategy to defeat the giants in your life. There is hope no matter what you have done or the road you've traveled. Don't get down on yourself because God set provision for our mistakes. I encourage you to use your testimony to help others break free. You breaking free of bondage can be someone else's breakthrough. God needs you and the kingdom needs you. You deserve to live your best life.

II

"Time to take action."
BREAKING THE CURSES

By now you should have an understanding of what curses are and how they affect your life. There is a full-out war being waged against the prosperity and miracles which were assigned to you. Just to be clear, patty cake prayers do not break strongholds. Curses place a cap on their victims preventing them from living up to their full capacities. Many of us have lived a life of lack, some financially, others in their relationships of all sorts, and many in their respective career paths. Wherever you lack there is a solution and we're going to confront it head-on in the pages to come.

This world is run by Satanists, can we escape everything? No, but we can be vigilant and do our best not to come into covenant with things that keep us bound. The cars we drive and stores we frequent all have Satanic symbols. Does that mean we should not buy groceries, not drive our cars, or wear clothing? No, we should simply be aware so that we are not living blindly. Life is meant to be enjoyed. I am by no means a stuffy person. I do not believe that we as believers should be dead in spirit. This is one of the things I hate most about the misconception of what it means to be a believer. I love to dance, go out for a great meal with food and drinks. I wear swimsuits at the beach, you will not catch me wearing a huge cloak. I laugh a lot. I'm far from perfect and have to repent daily. I am far from the look of the traditional looking Christian but I believe in God and am striving to see Him someday. I have chosen to work on my relationship with God as opposed to beating myself up trying to follow the traditions of the church. That was the purpose of Jesus dying on the cross.

Now that we have that heavy information covered, we need to deal with the principles which help us right the wrong in our lives. Leviticus 26:40-42 states, "If they shall confess their iniquity, and the iniquity of their fathers, with their trespass which they trespassed against me, and that also they have walked contrary unto me; And that I also have walked contrary unto them, and have brought them into the land of their enemies; if then their uncircumcised hearts be humbled, and they then accept of the punishment of their iniquity: Then will I remember my covenant with Jacob, and also my covenant with Isaac, and also my covenant with Abraham will I remember; and I will remember the land."

Will I continue to make mistakes? Absolutely, but I don't want to turn my poor decisions into a lifestyle. There's grace for mistakes but to continue in sin separates us from God, leading us to hell. "Well then, should we keep on sinning so that God can show us more and more of His wonderful grace?" (Romans 6:1). "Truly, I say to you, whatever you bind on Earth shall be bound in heaven, and whatever you loose on Earth shall be loosed in heaven," (Matthew 18:18).

FASTING

Fasting is something that believers do to shift the focus from what's going on in our natural state to petition God spiritually. This is a time where we humble ourselves before God, setting aside our plates to hunger and thirst after righteousness. Additionally, we fast to evoke spiritual help from Christ Jesus and the angelic host which was assigned to us at birth. Many people are reluctant to fast because it requires a sacrifice that many are not willing to undertake. But just as it is necessary to detox our physical bodies, so too is it necessary for our spirit.

While I renounced my membership with Delta Sigma Theta in the due form, I still had to take it up spiritually. As the physical process was underway, I needed to go deeper in Christ to spiritually break the evil covenants made at the Satanic altars. You should understand before going on a fast that you will gain a deeper insight into what is happening in the spiritual realm through dreams, visions, and general communication with the Holy Spirit. As those evil covenants are being broken, Satan is not letting go without a fight so you must understand that it will be spiritual warfare during and after your fast. The angels rejoice when one soul comes to Christ but Satan and his disciples become aggressively angry and will fight for you to remain in the world of darkness.

When you are doing everything right unto God, Satan will tempt you and make you feel as if everything is now wrong. You would think that when you're breaking these evil covenants that there will be cake, balloons, and congratulations but I am a witness that it is the exact opposite. Satan will try to suppress you through car trouble, issues in your relationships and on your job, financial lack, or even an attack on your body. You need to know his schemes so that you stay the course. It's like going to the gym to lose weight but you see the scale go up, making you discouraged. What you need to be aware of is that you're gaining muscle not fat, that is when trusting the process is of extreme importance.

I wish someone would have told me of the attacks that would form as opposed to being blindsided. I believe sometimes it's not the impact of the hit that hurts the most but rather the shock factor behind it all. An off-guard punch allows no room for bracing. I've found that keeping it real with people keeps them pursuing God. I have always hated gimmicks. As opposed to giving folks a pseudo-hope that causes them to lose faith I would rather equip God's people with the necessary tools to fight and win. You're gonna take some blows but they will be worth the freedom and victory that lies ahead.

Let's examine Daniel 9:3-19, which states, "So I turned to the Lord God and pleaded with Him in prayer and petition, in fasting, and in sackcloth and ashes. I prayed to the LORD my God and confessed: Lord, the great and awesome God, who keeps His covenant of love with those who love Him and keep His commandments, we have sinned and done wrong. We have been wicked and have rebelled; we have turned away from your commands and laws." This scripture taps into the very essence of what it means to fast. Fasting is a time to pray and confess our sins before God for us to be delivered. To deny ourselves of fleshly desires and seek the face of God is true humility before Him. Some of us have had deep dark secrets that we've lived with for years and have never uttered a word to a soul regarding those things. Vulnerability and transparency are key. It is vital to own the fact that we've sinned and fallen short of the glory of God. Confess the ancestral curses and ask for forgiveness for the offense that those who came before you committed. Come before the throne of grace boldly and break every evil covenant that you have entered into knowingly or unknowingly. Acts 13:2 shows how the Holy Spirit speaks as one sacrifice through fasting. "While they were worshiping the Lord and fasting, the Holy Spirit said, set apart for me Barnabas and Saul for the work to which I have called them."

If Jesus fasted forty days and forty nights to prepare for His three-year ministry, then we should know that this too is a requirement of ours. Fasting opens your spirit to receive divine impartations from God. Satan understands that and just as he tempted Jesus, we too will be tempted. If you can recall the chain of events, Satan first tempts Jesus by trying to get Him not to trust God. Secondly, Satan tries to get Jesus to test God, and Satan's last attempt was to offer Jesus the world in exchange to have Him bow to the authority of Satan. Satan was trying to entice Jesus with things the world was already enslaved by but Jesus' mission was bigger. Sin had no power over Christ. Although He had been sent from God to dwell in a physical vessel, Jesus still denied Himself to receive power from on high. He overcame Satan by calling back the word of God to counter every wicked tactic the devil tried to bring Him into bondage with, and that is what we must do as believers as well.

HOW LONG SHOULD YOU FAST?

The truth is, no one can tell you how long your fast should be because it is a sacrifice you are making to God. A fast can be for hours, days, weeks, or even months. Just as we detox our bodies, it is important to detox our spirits as needed. I believe one should fast as often as possible and as long as necessary. There are many different types of fasts. The most noted is a dry fast where you would not consume food or water for the time frame you have chosen to engage in the fast. There are water fasts and many more that others engage in as well. When breaking covenants that have kept you bound there should be a willingness to deny yourself for the sake of reaching higher ground spiritually and naturally. Seek God for the answer to how long your fast should be because every demonic force will require a different level of sacrifice. For me, the more I heard the voice of God the longer I wanted to stay on my fast and the more often I evoked one. Coming off my fasts I always feel elevated, almost as if I'm in a different dimension than the rest of the world. Spiritual law is spiritual law no matter if used for good or evil, this is why people in the world of the occult fast, so their gods can impart more unto them. As believers, this is a game-changer and makes the spirit realm clear as opposed to operating from a carnal perspective. In Delta, the entire process is known as a purification process. When I was pledging, certain foods were encouraged to be dismissed from one's diet, this is so the spirit of Minerva (Satan) can take over while the pyramid is at its purest form.

"Go, gather together all the Jews who are in Susa, and fast for me. Do not eat or drink for three days, night or day. I and my attendants will fast as you do. When this is done, I will go to the king, even though it is against the law. And if I perish, I perish," (Esther 4:16). In this scripture, Queen Esther called a three-day dry fast amongst the Jews because she had been enlisted by her uncle Mordecai to help save the Jews as Haman sought to destroy all the Jews. Queen Esther, unbeknownst to her husband King Ahasuerus, was a Jew. The destruction of her people could potentially mean the destruction of herself as well. She would have to approach her husband without being called, which was against the law and could result in her death. The three-day fast she called for changed the destiny of the Jews. Instead of death and destruction, they received honor and promotion. They used their spiritual weapons to defeat a battle they would otherwise lose.

Another account of the results of fasting is told by the prophet Ezra. "There, by the Ahava Canal, I proclaimed a fast, so that we might humble ourselves before our God and ask Him for a safe journey for us and our children, with all our possessions. I was ashamed to ask the king for soldiers and horsemen to protect us from enemies on the road, because we had told the king, 'The gracious hand of our God is on everyone who looks to Him, but His great anger is against all who forsake Him.' So we fasted and petitioned our God about this, and He answered our prayer," (Ezra 8:21-23).

HOW SHOULD WE FAST?

"And when you fast, do not look gloomy like the hypocrites, for they disfigure their faces that their fasting may be seen by others. Truly, I say to you, they have received their reward. But when you fast, anoint your head and wash your face, that your fasting may not be seen by others but by your Father, who is in secret. And your Father, who sees in secret will reward you," (Matthew 6:16-18). Here the Lord shows us that we should evoke a fast with a pure heart and spirit. Not to seek acknowledgment from people but rather spiritual enlightenment and help from God.

Just as it is sometimes a struggle to start something we are unfamiliar with, I am aware that some do not know the steps to take towards prayer. What I learned in the world of the occult is everything is written in guideline form so that whatever you are doing can be effective. In Christianity, I feel we lack because very few take the time to give practical application, many believe throwing out information is the end all be all. We would never feed a newborn baby steak, instead, we'd allow them to nurse off milk until they've matured to the next level. I believe we must take more care of God's people because many are lost and have been deceived. It is going to take prayer and patience to break folks from the strongholds they are in.

PRAYING

"Likewise the Spirit also helpeth our infirmities: for we know not what we should pray for as we ought: but the Spirit itself maketh intercession for us with groanings which cannot be uttered,"
(Romans 8:26).

Always allow the Holy Spirit to lead you in your prayers. He will give you the utterance. These prayers are designed to help you focus your prayers and pack your prayers with the word of God. God responds to His word so it is important to put Him in remembrance of what He has said. The angelic host assigned to your life will also be dispatched to cover you and work on your behalf by God's spoken word. So we must speak the word of God over our lives as much as possible because the word of God is our spiritual weapon. "For the word of God is quick, and powerful, and sharper than any two-edged sword, piercing even to the dividing asunder of soul and spirit, and of the joints and marrow, and is a discerner of the thoughts and intents of the heart," (Hebrews 4:12). Jesus also teaches us how to pray in Matthew 6:9-13, which outlines the Lord's Prayer.

Our Father, who art in heaven,
hallowed be thy name;
thy kingdom come;
thy will be done;
on Earth as it is in heaven.

Give us this day our daily bread.
And forgive us our trespasses,
as we forgive those who trespass against us.
And lead us not into temptation;
but deliver us from evil.
For thine is the kingdom,
the power and the glory,
for ever and ever.
Amen.

Please do not make the mistake of believing you have to finesse God to get a response. Develop a relationship with Him based on truth and transparency. He knows your thoughts and motives so be straight up with God. My relationship with God may differ from the "religious" teachings on how to pray because I communicate with God about how I feel, what I am going through, and how I need His help to do everything, including breathing. After all, He is my Father. Matthew 6:5 states, "And when you pray, do not be like the hypocrites. For they love to pray standing in the synagogues and on the street corners to be seen by men. Truly I tell you, they already have their full reward." Contrary to popular beliefs, the most effective prayers can happen in your shower, while driving, or even in the silence of your being.

Mark 11:22-25 reminds us of principles we must adhere to before praying. It states, "Have faith in God," Jesus said to them. "Truly I tell you that if anyone says to this mountain, 'Be lifted up and thrown into the sea,' and has no doubt in his heart but believes that it will happen, it will be done for him. Therefore I tell you, whatever you ask for in prayer, believe that you have received it, and it will be yours. And when you stand to pray, if you hold anything against another, forgive it, so that your Father in heaven will forgive your trespasses as well." This scripture outlines that a prerequisite for prayer is having a clean heart free from bitterness, strife, and unforgiveness.

Opposite of what most want to believe, God will not honor your prayers while harboring hidden things in your heart so we must deal with that first. Secondly, we must have faith that we will receive whatever we are requesting according to the laws of God before we even utter the words in prayer. Fear is the ultimate enemy of faith. You cannot believe that God can and will in one moment, then be easily persuaded otherwise the next minute. I understand that the enemy will ride you and attack you on every hand but this is the importance of calling God's word back to Him and that is what the prayers outlined in this book will assist you in doing.

ACCEPTING GOD'S WILL THROUGH DREAM & RENOUNCING EVIL DREAMS

As said, dreams are the eye-gate to the spirit realm. Each time I go to sleep, be it for a night's rest or a quick nap, I have now made it a habit to suit myself in the full armor of God calling each piece of the armor over myself. By far, the most powerful prayer we can pray is the one we utter when awaking in the morning or from a dream. We can see in several scriptural accounts where God spoke to people in their dreams: Abraham, Jacob, Joseph, Solomon, Pilate's wife, and scores of others. Let's hone in on the account of Abraham when he was called Abram: "Now when the sun was going down, a deep sleep fell upon Abram; and behold, horror and great darkness fell upon him. Then he said to Abram: 'Know certainly that your descendants will be strangers in a land that is not theirs and will serve them, and they will afflict them four hundred years. And also the nation whom they serve I will judge; afterward, they shall come out with great possessions. Now as for you, you shall go to your fathers in peace; you shall be buried at a good old age. But in the fourth generation, they shall return here, for the iniquity of the Amorites is not yet complete," (Genesis 15:12-16).

We can see how God speaks prophetically through dreams. God gets human consent before He allows things to manifest on Earth. Satan does the same thing and will oftentimes do it deceptively and in our dreams. A prime example is in Matthew 13:25, which states, "But while men slept, his enemy came and sowed tares among the wheat, and went his way." This shows how Satan waits for the opportunity to deceive people in their unconscious state. The physical body is asleep but the spirit is awake. Many people get up from a dream, good or bad, and do not internalize what has taken place. Some will say it was a scattered dream and didn't make sense or that they remember some things but not enough to make sense of it.

Regardless, it is important to make a habit of writing down your dreams with dates, times, and as many details as possible. You must pray about the dreams you are having and petition God for the interpretations of these dreams as well. It is perfectly normal not to understand everything you dream about. That is why we can see biblical accounts where one would dream and another would be able to interpret what God was saying. Joseph in Genesis 37:5-11 had a dream: "Joseph had a dream, and when he told it to his brothers, they hated him all the more. He said to them, 'Listen to this dream I had: We were binding sheaves of grain out in the field when suddenly my sheaf rose and stood upright, while your sheaves gathered around mine and bowed down to it.' His brothers said to him, 'Do you intend to reign over us? Will you actually rule us?' And they hated him all the more because of his dream and what he had said. Then he had another dream, and he told it to his brothers. 'Listen,' he said, 'I had another dream, and this time the sun and moon and eleven stars were bowing down to me.' When he told his father as well as his brothers, his father rebuked him and said, 'What is this dream you had? Will your mother and I and your brothers actually come and bow down to the ground before you?' His brothers were jealous of him, but his father kept the matter in mind."

Joseph did not indicate that he understood his dreams then, but his brothers and father certainly had the gift of interpretation. God was showing Joseph that of his entire family, he would be in a place of leadership and that they would all bow to him in honor. As Joseph went on to be sold into slavery, served in another land, thrown in prison falsely, God began to pour

His spirit out more on Joseph and he received favor no matter where he was. Although it is clear that Joseph did not initially understand his dream, God would later give him the interpretation of the King's baker and cupbearer's dreams. Later he also interpreted a dream for the King which prophetically warned of seven years of harvest and seven years of famine. That dream alone saved the land of Egypt, making them the wealthiest of all the lands. The gift was always in Joseph but spiritual maturity was developed and led him to become the second most powerful man in all of Egypt, a land that was not his native home. That should give you an indication of just how powerful and prophetic dreams are. We'll now dive into some prayers that will help you break strongholds and live in God's abundance.

PRAYERS

A Prayer to pray when waking up:

Father God, I thank you for waking me up and clothing me in my right mind. God as I slept, I am not sure of every aspect of my dreams. God, I come into full agreement with your will as you have said according to Jeremiah 29:11 that you have plans to prosper me and not harm me, to give me hope and a future and I believe your word. But Father God, if the enemy deceptively crept in while I slept then I reject, rebuke, and renounce every evil covenant he has sought to forge with me. His assignment is to steal, kill, and destroy and I do not consent to any of his wicked schemes. I thank you for allowing me to see into the spirit realm and ask you to give further clarity on these dreams. In Jesus' name, I pray, Amen.

BREAKING GENERATIONAL CURSES

Dear Heavenly Father, I come to you today asking for your forgiveness for the sins that I've committed against you and for the sins of my ancestors. You warned us in scripture that you are "a jealous God, punishing the children for the sin of the fathers to the third and fourth generation of those who hate you." Lord, we've disobeyed you and rebelled against your word. Please forgive us. Today I turn away from false idols and all of the Satanic things that are not of you and cleave to your word. You promised that if I come near you, you will come near me. Lord, I'm coming to you as a sinner and asking you to wash and purify my heart.

Help me Lord to become stronger in you so I do not repeat the sins of my fathers. According to your word in 2 Chronicles 7:14, "if My people, who are called by My name, shall humble themselves and pray, and seek My face and turn from their wicked ways, then will I hear from heaven, and will forgive their sin and will heal their land." Father, I am trusting that you will heal me and restore everything that the devil stole. Break every curse that has me bound and send your holy fire to burn every evil altar that was set up against me and my family's destiny. I reject every demonic spirit permeating curses and speaking to my destiny from the evil altars set up by my ancestors.

I break the spirits of fear, poverty, anger, negativity, promiscuity, barrenness, non-marriage, divorce, abuse, addictions, incest, perversion, rape, homosexuality, non-progress, mental illnesses, physical sickness, murderous spirits, lying, gossiping, stealing, repossession, profanity, perverse speaking, and all other ungodly spirits that seek to control my life and the lives of my family members. Lord, I acknowledge you as the supreme being, the one and only true living God. You are the head of my life and I put no other god before you. You wish that I prosper in all that I do, realign me, Lord, to the perfect will that you set for me before the foundation of this world. I believe that I am forgiven and healed by your blood. I thank you Jesus for your grace and mercy. I am FREE in Christ Jesus. I will walk in the abundance that you've set before me from this day forth in Jesus' name Amen.

FINANCIAL PROSPERITY

Father God, I come before you humbly acknowledging your supreme being. You are God, the God of our Father Abraham whom you promised to make a great nation with wealth, good health, spiritual prosperity, and abundance. So God I come to you reminding you of your covenant. Father God, you said in your word according to Proverbs 11:24-25, "One person gives freely, yet gains even more; another withholds unduly, but comes to poverty, a generous person will prosper; whoever refreshes others will be refreshed." Well Father God I have refreshed your people for years and on this day and in this year, I am requesting a financial refresher and release from you. Father God just as your word states in Nehemiah 2:20, "The God of heaven will give us success."

Jesus I am depending on you to launch me spiritually and financially in this hour, on this day, and in this year. Lord, send forth the rain in my life. Jehovah-Jireh my provider, do as you promised to do in Deuteronomy 28:11-12, "to make me plenteous in goods, in the fruit of my body, and in the fruit of my cattle, and in the fruit of my ground, in the land you swore to give to our Fathers." God grant me these things along with the wisdom that I may steward well over all the things you have given me spiritually, physically, and financially. I believe in the power and might of my Lord and Savior Jesus Christ, so it is in that power I rely on. Let me not be as Pagans to worry about what I will eat, drink or wear but allow me to walk in your promise according to Deuteronomy 15:6, "For the Lord, your God will bless you as He has promised and you will lend to many nations but will borrow from none. You will rule over many nations but none will rule over you."

I bind myself to your word and your promises, and the laws you have established for your chosen people. I speak to my finances and command that all financial blessings and breakthroughs come forth right now in Jesus' name. All delays and setbacks on my pending financial blessings are canceled in the name of Jesus. Overflow come forth, abundance come forth, prosperity come forth. Lord, re-establish and reinstate me as a law-abiding citizen of the kingdom of heaven. In Jesus' matchless name I pray, Amen!

Proverbs 10:22, "The blessings of the Lord brings wealth without painful toil for it."

Lord, allow me to never work until the point of exhaustion unto man, knowing that my Father promised blessings without pain.

Psalms 145:16, "Thou openest thine hand and satisfies the desires of every living thing."

Father God, satisfy my desires. You know every need in my life. By faith, I believe I lack nothing because you will open your hand in due season.

Proverbs 21:5, "The plans of the diligent lead to profit, as surely as haste leads to poverty."

Lord please calm my spirit and let me be anxious for nothing. For my desire is to be profitable, prosperous, and diligent in all I do unto you.

HEALTH

Jehovah Rapha you are the God who heals. Lord, I come before you to repent of my sins and ask that you create in me a clean heart that I may serve you. I am fully aware that my sin will cause mental and physical sickness to overtake my body so I ask that you heal me of any sin you may find within me. Point out each area of my life where I lack your spirit and strengthen me to turn from my wicked ways. Lord, you said in your word according to Exodus 15:26, if I diligently heed to the voice of the Lord my God and do what is right in His sight, give ear to His commandments and keep all His statutes, then you will put none of the diseases on me. For you are the Lord who heals me. Well, God, I take you at your word, I come against any levied curses or attacks on my bloodstream, my body, my limbs, my scalp, my hair, my sight, my hearing, my tastebuds, my ability to feel and think with a sound mind. I reject and rebuke any parasites, funguses, or cancers and cast them back in the pits of hell where they belong.

God your servant David said, "I am fearfully and wonderfully made," and I believe that you have made us perfect in your sight. Jehovah Rapha, heal this body and mind and make it function the way you originally intended before my sins and before the foundations of the Earth. Father

God, just as you healed and added years to King Hezekiah's life in 2 Kings 2:20, after he cried out to you and called back how he has kept your commandments and done what was right in your eyes, I petition you to do the same for me. Lord, restore the years that the locusts and cankerworm have eaten up in my life as you promised according to Joel 2:25. By faith, I believe you've heard my cry and answered my prayers. No matter what is presented before me I will hold fast to the faith you've given me. In Jesus' name. Amen

RELATIONSHIPS

God, I thank you for sending your son Jesus Christ to bear the curse of all sins on the cross that I may have life and have it more abundantly. You showed your unfailing love then and keep showing it daily by breathing life into me. Father God, I desire a better relationship with you. I do not want to live this life without you or make decisions on my own. I need your help. You said in your word that you would show grace to those who love you and I want you to know I love you. I need your help with the relationships I am in. I need your strength and revelation to help me see spiritually what my carnal eyes cannot see. I am seeking wisdom to balance this all and you said according to James 1:5 if any man seeks wisdom we should ask and you will give it to us generously.

Lord, open your hand and pour your spirit upon me and every relationship I am in. Set your holy fire to burn up every relationship I am not meant to be in and comfort my heart as I have to let go. God, I seek to be a better child and servant to you and wear your seal but I cannot do that while being entangled in stressful relationships. God, I put my entire family before you, my husband/wife, my children, my friends, co-workers, business partners, investors, church leaders, sisters and brothers in Christ, whether they are here now or pending spiritually. I am asking you to work in my relationships in such a miraculous way that the world understands we are called by your name.

Lord, you said that believers should not be unequally yoked so align my relationships. Untie me from any relationship that separates me from my devotion to you. Help me to respect and treat well the people you've placed in my life and empower them to do the same. Lord convict my spirit severely if I ever make anyone an idol and help me to swiftly renounce and repent of my wicked ways. I declare and decree that every spirit of pride be cast down by the power and might of my Lord and Savior Jesus Christ. I plead the blood of Jesus over my relationships. I release humility, unity, forgiveness, healing, transparency, the love of God, and mercy into all my relationships right now in Jesus' name. Lord, you said in your word according to Isaiah 54:17 no weapon formed against me will prevail, and every tongue that accuses me shall be condemned. This is the heritage of the servants of the Lord, and this is my vindication, declares the Lord.

Right now I command the angelic host assigned to me to be dispatched to the four corners of this Earth and in the heavenly realm to fight for me and the original will God had for my life before the foundations of the Earth. I speak to my relationships and say be as they were meant to be before sin and corruption took form. I bless your name God because I know you have heard my prayer and will honor this as it is, in accordance to your will that I prosper even as my soul prospers in Jesus' matchless name. Amen

UNFAIRNESS/ REJECTION

Father God, I come to you as many things are happening in my life that are wicked and unjust. Lord, I am doing everything I know how to stay humble and allow you to work these situations out on my behalf. You see (insert situation, specific names of people, corporations, etc) and because you are a righteous God you are fully aware that this is unfair and far from just in your eyes. Just as King David prayed in Psalms 25:2, God I come to you letting you know that I trust you, do not let me be disgraced and put to shame and do not let my enemies rejoice in my defeat. God your justice is perfect. In your righteousness, you made the heavens and the Earth, so surely these situations I am facing are no match to you. "O let the evil of the wicked come to an end, but establish the righteous; For the righteous God tries the hearts and minds," (Psalms 7:9). Father God, I am aware that the enemy wishes to sift me like wheat but you Lord are my strong tower. You promise to set up a hedge of protection over me in Psalms 91 and I am calling your word back to you. In this hour and on this day I call forth the angels that encamp around me to wage war on my behalf.

Lord, allow your ministering angels to speak to me because I need to know the hidden things you wish to reveal to me. Allow my heart and spirit to receive and move according to the words that will be ministered. I cast down by the power of Jesus Christ every lying tongue, every plot, scheme, and trick of the enemy to be null and void and of no effect in my life. Right now, I release the truth, peace, a sound mind, wholeness, and healing over my life. No weapon formed against me shall prosper in the mighty name of Jesus. Let these words take root in the spirit realm to manifest here on Earth. Jesus, you paid the ultimate price on the cross and purchased my freedom so I am standing on the passion you've shown for me to know you're going to work on my behalf. Lord these people have stolen time, energy, promotions, and peace of mind from me. According to Proverbs 6:31, if the thief is found then he must pay back seven times what he stole, even if he has to sell everything in his house. Because of the injustice I have faced, Lord, I ask that you bless me sevenfold beyond what human eyes can see, launching me into the place that I should have been at this time. I call forth a supernatural release of forgiveness, comfort, restoration, new beginnings, the vengeance of God, and honor for your name's sake. Thank you God, for hearing me and answering my requests. Blessings will flow from this point forward because I am binding myself to your word and your law. In Jesus' name, I pray, Amen.

Acknowledgements

I want to sincerely thank God for sending the Holy Spirit to empower the words of this book.

Everything flowed effortlessly because the power of God orchestrated it that way. I extend my sincerest gratitude to the Executive Producer of the Crys Speaks brand, my prayer partner, sister, and best friend, Chanice. Chanice you've been the wind beneath my wings and saw the potential in me when I didn't always see it in myself. You've prayed with me during my darkest hours, turned down your plate to invoke fasts with me that broke chains over my life and you've been the epitome of a true sister and friend. God had me in mind when He created you and for that I thank Him. Despite the challenges and struggles, we stuck with God and the God of heaven has given us success to continue to build His kingdom. Everything you do for me and for the Crys Speaks fan base at large is greatly appreciated. May it serve as a credit to your spiritual account. May all that you do continue to flourish as God blesses your gifts and talents all the more.

To my friend and sister Bianca, thank you for your willingness to invest in this project without even knowing what I was writing about. I told you my plan to share my story with the world and your words were, "let's do it, I want to help. It would be my pleasure to invest into my sister who has the gift of hearing from God. Whatever it takes I got you." When you first found me you were very clear that God had sent you to help me but you were not sure in what way He was going to use you to administer that help. I'm assured that God sent you in my life for such a time as this.

You've been real and stayed real and for that, I send my heartfelt love to you. You've been the unsung hero behind some of the greatest talents the world has seen and I would be remiss if I did not take this time to publicly thank you for your pure heart and genuine spirit. For the blessings you render privately, may God advance you publicly in all that you do my friend.

Finally, to every Crys Speaks fan that follows me on my respective social media platforms, thank you for the continuous outpouring of love after all of these years. Every like, share, and comment is truly appreciated. I pray over you all often and I know that God is sending blessings to each of you as you align with His will. Thank you guys for allowing me to be my authentic self, for experiencing the highs and lows with me, and for calling my name out to God. I want you to know those prayers are keeping me. You all have pressed for a book and God has finally approved me to release it. I pray that it brings more healing, empowerment, and enlightenment to you. To my "Royals," the best is yet to come. Let's go higher in God together. Zion is our promise. As always, I love you much my love. The blessings of God are upon us.

Afterword:

After facing spiritual and physical identity theft, living nearly a decade in a curse, and having everything stripped from me, I am proud to now be in my rightful position in the kingdom of God. To live a life of freedom means the world to me; I have fought long and hard for my birthright. My relationships are thriving. My businesses and finances are flourishing and my spirit is redeemed. I feel like a huge weight has been lifted from me.

These days I move very carefully. After having been deceived and defying the will of God, that place of bondage I was in is a space I never want to revisit. I was once in the wilderness. God reinstated me as an heir to the promised land. I learned to use the word of God to tear down strongholds and to speak life into my situations. I once believed that prayer would solve everything. I discovered that fasting and speaking the word of God is a game-changer. I have learned how to arrest things spiritually before they manifest on Earth and speak to my destiny according to the laws of God.

My faith in God has increased. I have seen His hand work out situations that seem impossible to man. The spirit realm is not something to manipulate. I have learned to allow my creator to lead me down the path He created for me before the foundations of the Earth. Manifesting the life I desired led me down the road of destruction. My thirst and hunger for the things of the Lord have grown immensely. As the saying goes, it is impossible to come in contact with God and remain the same. Spreading the good news of God is like going to a good restaurant, traveling to a beautiful location, or having a breath-taking moment. If you are anything like me, you want everyone to experience it and somehow taste the grace. I am far from perfect. Just like you, I have my moments. I am constantly striving. The enemy fights me but I have learned to dispatch my angelic host because the victory has already been won.

I enjoy laughing out loud, traveling, dancing like nobody's watching, wine tastings, and experiencing the fullness of this Earth. I'm not a stuffy person. I believe there is room to have a personality while fulfilling your God-ordained purpose. Above all else, I pray that the pages of this book provoke you to seek God more for the spiritual understanding you need to break the curses that may have you bound and to develop an intimate relationship with your Father God. I also pray that you hide the word of God in your heart and do as much as possible to live according to it so that we live in the abundance He predestined for us. Lack and slavery was never our birthright.

Elohim Save Us!

SPEAK ON IT...

Notes:

_____
_____
_____
_____
_____
_____
_____
_____
_____
_____
_____
_____
_____
_____
_____

SPEAK ON IT...

Notes:
_____
_____
_____
_____
_____
_____
_____
_____
_____
_____
_____
_____
_____
_____
_____
_____
_____
_____

SPEAK ON IT...

Notes:

_____
_____
_____
_____
_____
_____
_____
_____
_____
_____
_____
_____
_____
_____
_____
_____
_____

SPEAK ON IT...

Notes:

_____
_____
_____
_____
_____
_____
_____
_____
_____
_____
_____
_____
_____
_____
_____

SPEAK ON IT...

Notes:

_____
_____
_____
_____
_____
_____
_____
_____
_____
_____
_____
_____
_____
_____
_____
_____
_____

SPEAK ON IT...

Notes:

_____
_____
_____
_____
_____
_____
_____
_____
_____
_____
_____
_____
_____
_____
_____

SPEAK ON IT...

Notes:

_____
_____
_____
_____
_____
_____
_____
_____
_____
_____
_____
_____
_____
_____
_____

SPEAK ON IT...

Notes:

_____
_____
_____
_____
_____
_____
_____
_____
_____
_____
_____
_____
_____
_____
_____

Works Cited

"3 Hidden Meanings of Number 5 in the Bible." Numerology Nation, 5 July 2021, numerologynation.com/numerology/biblical/number-5/.

"Alchemy." Merriam-Webster, Merriam-Webster, www.merriam-webster.com/dictionary/alchemy.

Bard, Síle the. "The Pentagram and THE Pentacle: What You Should Know." Which Witches, 20 July 2020, whichwitches.com/2020/07/19/the-pentagram-and-the-pentacle-what-you-should-know/.

"Blood Wings." Wikipedia, Wikimedia Foundation, 13 May 2021, en.wikipedia.org/wiki/Blood_wings.

Bradford, Alina. "The Five (and More) Senses." LiveScience, Purch, 24 Oct. 2017, www.livescience.com/60752-human-senses.html.

"Cern Accelerating Science." Home, home.cern/.

"Charis (Name)." Wikipedia, Wikimedia Foundation, 15 Aug. 2021, en.wikipedia.org/wiki/Charis_(name).

Codex Magica —16, www.bibliotecapleyades.net/sociopolitica/codex_magica/codex_magica16.htm.

"Dark Matter." Wikipedia, Wikimedia Foundation, 12 Aug. 2021, en.wikipedia.org/wiki/Dark_matter.

"Death March." Wikipedia, Wikimedia Foundation, 20 July 2021, https://en.wikipedia.org/wiki/Death_march

"Elephant Symbolism & Meaning: SPIRIT, Totem, & Power Animal." What Is My Spirit Animal | Spirit, Totem, & Power Animals, 6 July 2021, whatismyspiritanimal.com/spirit-totem-power-animal-meanings/mammals/elephant-symbolism-meaning/.

"Esoteric Definition & Meaning." Dictionary.com, Dictionary.com, https://www.dictionary.com/browse/esoteric

"Greek Life." Montclair State University https://www.montclair.edu/greek-life/

Greek Word for Satisfaction. climatesystemsllc.com/wp-content/uploads/formidable/4/greek-word-for-satisfaction.pdf.

"Hermetic Order of the Golden Dawn." Wikipedia, Wikimedia Foundation, 17 July 2021, en.wikipedia.org/wiki/Hermetic_Order_of_the_Golden_Dawn.

"How Are Ships Named —Naming and Launching Ceremony." Google, Google, www.google.com/amp/s/www.marineinsight.com/life-at-sea/how-are-ships-named-naming-and-launching-ceremony/amp/.

"Magic Circle." Wikipedia, Wikimedia Foundation, 15 June 2021, en.wikipedia.org/wiki/Magic_circle.

"Muses." Wikipedia, Wikimedia Foundation, 4 Aug. 2021, en.wikipedia.org/wiki/Muses.

"Pentagram." Headhunter's Horror House Wiki, headhuntershorrorhouse.fandom.com/wiki/Pentagram.

The Pyramids of Mexico — Watchtower Online Library — JW.ORG. wol.jw.org/en/wol/d/r1/lp-e/102000730.

Ryan, Ash. "The True Stories and Meanings behind Nursery Rhymes and Lullabies." WeHaveKids, WeHaveKids, 19 Oct. 2014, wehavekids.com/education/The-True-Stories-and-Meanings-Behind-Nursery-Rhymes-and-Lullabies.

"Satanic/Occult Symbols and Their Meanings." https://static1.squarespace.com/static/52a5ddbae4b0ea452efcfe32/t/5c37c3851ae6cfc0093c814f/1547158406535/Satanic+and+Occult+symbols+updated+May+2018.pdf

Glossary

Ace—The first person in the pledge class' line.

Brother—Term that fraternity members call each other.

Call/Chant—A yell used mostly by Greeks used to identify and greet brothers and sisters. Emulating a call/chant is a sign of disrespect.

Chapter—A branch of a national sorority, established at a campus. Each will have their own name, usually designated by Greek letters.

Chapter Meeting—A meeting held to discuss fraternity or sorority business.

Colors—The official pair or triad of colors that represent a specific Greek organization.

Financial—Term used to refer to an active member. (i.e. a dues-paying member).

Crest—Insignia used by fraternity or sorority members. Most Greek organizations reserve the crest for initiated members only. Each crest has hidden, secret meanings behind it.

Crossed—The date on which an associate member crossed into a fraternity or sorority to become an active member. Usually, a term used in culturally-centered Greek organizations.

Divine Nine—A nickname for the nine historically African American Greek organizations on the National Pan-Hellenic Council.

Dean of Pledge—Person who oversees the membership intake process.

Dues—Charge for joining a fraternity or sorority. Covers costs of national and local operations, formal events, activities and other events. The amount varies based on the organization.

Founders—The establishing members of the organization.

Fraternity—A group of people brought together because of mutual interests. Generally thought of as a group of men, but also refers to co-ed organizations and many sororities are officially fraternities.

Greek—Not the nationality. Greek in this sense means a member of a Greek letter fraternity or sorority.

Greeting—Greetings are defined as formalized ways in which a potential new member is required to address a current member of the organization in which skits, songs, prose, etc. are incorporated.

Handshake—It's a special handshake unique to each organization. Only initiated members will know the handshake. Also known as a 'grip'.

Hazing—Any act performed by a member of any organization that is likely to cause harm or danger, cause public embarrassment or shame, compromise a person's dignity, cause the person to be the object of ridicule, cause psychological harm, or is illegal.

Inactive— Members of an organization who are not financially active or in some cases physically active.

Initiate—A person who has recently learned the ritual of a fraternity or sorority and is a full member.

Initiation—A ceremony where a pledge/prospective new member becomes a full member of the organization. Initiation ceremonies are private and different for all organizations.

Legacy—The son, daughter, brother or sister of an organization's member. Some organizations also include grandchildren or stepchildren. Sorority rules sometimes dictate she cannot be cut from the first round of parties, but in no way are legacies guaranteed a bid from the organization they are a legacy to.

Letters—The first Greek letter of each Greek word that makes up the name of the fraternity or sorority are often displayed on clothing.

Line—A National Pan Hellenic Council (NPHC) term somewhat equal to a pledge/new member class. They are the potential new members of the organization. Lines are often given names called ship names.

Marching—Marching is defined as but is not limited to potential new members linked arm in arm, stepping or stomping loudly in unison, dipping and/or chanting/singing.

Mascot—A symbol (official/non official), usually an animal, chosen to represent a Greek letter organization.

Neophyte aka Neo— New member of Greek Letter organization; also called a 'Neo'. This term is generally used by NPHC organizations.

New Member Pin—A distinctive badge worn on the chest designating a new member of a particular fraternity or sorority for the period of time between acceptance and initiation. Most organizations require the new member to return the new member pin at initiation in exchange for their official member pin.

New Member Class—The group of new members that will be going through the New Member Program and Initiation together. Formerly called a pledge class, this term is still used among the fraternities. In Delta Sigma Theta Sorority, Incorporated, it is known as the Pyramids.

Number—The number you are assigned based on the chronological order you are in on your initiation line (often members of other culturally based organizations identify or relate to one another by distinguishing that they are the "same" number).

On the yard—Organizations refer to it as a chapter that is currently chartered on campus.

Paraphernalia—Also known as 'para' or 'nalia'. This is clothing and accessories which display the organization's letters.

Patron-The Greek god/goddess of the Greek letter organization.

Pin– The active pin is worn on the chest designating an initiated member of a certain chapter. A new member pin is similar and is used to designate a new member/potential new member of a chapter.

Pinning—Designates the start of a new member process. The new member wears a fraternity/sorority pin and at the moment of pinning, officially become a new member.

Pledgee—New member seeking to gain membership.

Probate/Coming Out Show—The new member's presentation to the campus usually done in masks or coverings of some sort to disguise identity until revealed.

Prophyte—A term used to describe an older member of an NPHC organization that has inducted new members.

Ritual—A secret ceremony of a Greek organization. Also, the formal document that contains the secret principles and ideals upon which the organization was founded. Ritual elements are sacred to each fraternity and sorority and have been handed down through generations. Only initiated members may be privy to rituals.

Sands—An NPHC term for members of your new member class or Greeks who became members the same semester. Comes from the phrase "cross the burning sands" which means to cross over (become initiated) into full membership.

Ship—Individuals who are members of the same intake class (line).

Sign—A unique display expressed by hand symbols, typically by NPHC organizations. Emulating the sign is a sign of disrespect.

Sister—Term that sorority members call each other.

Soror—Means sister, this is a term used by NPHC sorority members to acknowledge one another. Rarely used among PC sororities.

Sorority—A Greek organization for women.

Step Show—A show performed by NPHC organizations (as well as other organizations) which include a combination of stepping and strolling, among other activities.

Stepping—is a form of percussive dance in which the participant's entire body is used as an instrument to produce complex rhythms and sounds through a mixture of footsteps and handclaps.

Stroll(ing)—Also known as 'party walk(ing)' An energetic, synchronized dance. Typically, NPHC Organizational members move together in a line expressing pride for their organization. In this line, members may express their pride through use of their organization's call, sign or historical information, ritual/custom dances, etc. All of this is done through movements that are unique to a particular organization. Emulating or cutting in/through the line is considered a sign of disrespect.

Tail—The last person of the line.

Underground Pledging—A process by which the students are in with little to no communication with the general population.

Uniform—an identifying outfit or style of dress worn by the members/potential new members of a given organization.

(Greek Life)

About the Author

With all of her accomplishments, the greatest gift is her God-given ability to spiritually & physically heal. The testimonies of those she has helped are found in the comments of motivational videos on her social media platforms which reach millions of people worldwide every month. She believes that "Where much is given, much is required." After God saved her from a road leading to destruction, He gave her the commandment to "Free my people." Her mission is to help God's people in all facets of their life; it's beyond a profession, it's her purpose. Crys Speaks resides in Miami, Florida.

Visit Crys Speaks online at: www.crysspeaks.com
All Social Media Platforms: @CrysSpeaks

www.ingramcontent.com/pod-product-compliance
Lightning Source LLC
Chambersburg PA
CBHW071453070526
44578CB00001B/325